CrB

8

Knowledge and Society

AN INTRODUCTION
TO THE PHILOSOPHY
OF THE SOCIAL SCIENCES

Knowledge and Society

AN INTRODUCTION
TO THE PHILOSOPHY
OF THE SOCIAL SCIENCES

Arnold B. Levison

PEGASUS

A DIVISION OF

THE BOBBS-MERRILL COMPANY, INC., PUBLISHERS

Indianapolis   New York

This book is one of a series, Traditions in Philosophy, published in cooperation with Educational Resources Corporation, which created and developed the series under the direction of Nicholas Capaldi, Professor of Philosophy, Queens College, New York.

Library of Congress Cataloging in Publication Data

Levison, Arnold Boyd.
Knowledge and society.
(Traditions in philosophy)
1. Social sciences.   I. Title.

H61.L47   300'.1   72-88122
ISBN 0-672-53661-7
ISBN 0-672-63661-1 (pbk)

For Gulley and Jessie

Acknowledgments

The author is grateful for permission to quote from the following:

Hempel, Carl G., "Typological Methods in the Social Sciences," in *Science, Language and Human Rights*: The University of Pennsylvania Press, Philadelphia, 1952.

Inquiry, Vol. 9 (1966) : Universitetsforlaget, Oslo, Norway.

Mind, Vol. 78, No. 309: Basil Blackwell & Mott Ltd., Oxford, England.

Quine, Willard Van Orman, *Word and Object*: The Technology Press of the Massachusetts Institute of Technology and John Wiley & Sons, Inc., New York and London. Copyright © 1960 by The Massachusetts Institute of Technology.

Sellars, Wilfred, Introduction, "Intentionality and the Mental" from *Minnesota Studies in the Philosophy of Science, Volume II,* edited by H. Feigl, M. Scriven, and G. Maxwell: University of Minnesota Press, Minneapolis © 1958, University of Minnesota.

Smith, Norman Kemp, *Hume's Dialogues Concerning Natural Religion,* second edition: Macmillan, London and Basingstoke, and St. Martin's Press, Inc., New York, 1946.

Weber, Max, *The Theory of Social and Economic Organization,* translated and edited by A. M. Henderson and Talcott Parsons: The Macmillan Company. Copyright © 1947 by Talcott Parsons.

Winch, Peter, *The Idea of a Social Science*: Humanities Press, Inc., New York; and Routledge & Kegan Paul, Ltd., London, 1958.

Contents

Preface

This book discusses some central issues in the philosophy of social science, considered from the perspective of their historical development from Hume to the present. I attempted to make these issues intelligible to the general reader, but without watering down the problems or making the work useless for more advanced readers. This aim has dictated the organization of material. Historical issues are used as a vehicle for introducing contemporary problems, the earlier chapters providing preparation needed for understanding later ones.

The orientation of the book is epistemological rather than methodological. That is, I focus on the question, What kinds of knowledge, if any, are properly and characteristically produced by the social sciences? instead of the question, By what methods can the social sciences best achieve their aims? While many excellent treatments of methodological problems of the social sciences already exist, there are relatively few concerned with epistemology. Yet epistemological assumptions often determine methodological principle, and are philosophically more fundamental.

I have limited my attention to a few philosophers and social scientists whose views and styles of argument continue to influence philosophical thinking about the social sciences. For example, I devote an entire chapter to Hume, relatively little space to J. S. Mill, and none at all to Auguste Comte. Although Mill and Comte may have had more influence on the thinking of social scientists, Hume went more deeply into the epistemological problems relevant to social science and is a more original and forceful thinker than either Mill or Comte.

Furthermore, I discuss only those parts of a writer's views that seem to bear directly on my central questions, which are briefly summarized in the first chapter. I thought it better to discuss a few related issues thoroughly than a great many superficially. For treatments of other equally important issues in the philosophy of the social sciences, the reader should consult some of the books listed in the bibliography.

Many social scientists may object to my approach on grounds that the problems I consider are not relevant to any issues that are alive today in the social- or behavioral-science institutions. My defense is that epistemological problems of the sciences, natural as well as social, have always been irrelevant to research interests of scientists. They are problems whose solution affects not so much the science as our *understanding* of the science, and whose treatment requires the special training and methods of philosophers. The philosophy of a science may be approached in many different, equally legitimate ways, but it need not be restricted to questions whose answers would further the progress of that science.

Chapters VI through VIII are considerably more technical than preceding ones and are likely to cause the general reader more difficulty. I have included them because there seemed no other way of introducing basic issues in contemporary thought about the social sciences. These chapters should be read along with some of the primary source material referred to in the notes.

This book will have achieved its purpose if it helps to convince the reader that contemporary problems in the epistemology of social science are not arbitrary inventions of academic philosophers, but are products of a long period of historical germination and growth. Thus the prevalent belief in a sharp break or discontinuity between contemporary philosophical concerns and those of the philosophy of the past, is mistaken. The problems that troubled Hume are still very much with us, however different the language we use to discuss them, and however ramified the problem-areas have become since Hume's time. In the philosophy of the social sciences, as well as in other fields, the price of neglecting the thought of the past is a poorer understanding of the present.

I would like to thank Irving Thalberg, Jr., with whom I collaborated originally on much of the material contained in Chapter V, and my friends and former colleagues at Chicago Circle, especially Ruth Barcan Marcus, Terence Parsons, and Fred Feldman, who participated in many stimulating discussions about issues contained in this book. Thanks are also due H. Jane Braude, who not only typed the manuscript, but made many helpful editorial comments and suggestions.

Arnold Levison

If we contemplate the whole field of human knowledge, attained or attainable, we find that it separates itself obviously, and as it were spontaneously, into two divisions which stand so strikingly in opposition and contradistinction to one another that in all classifications of our knowledge they have been kept apart. These are *physical* science and *moral* or psychological sciences.

John Stuart Mill

I

Philosophy and
the Social Sciences

Introduction.

We are accustomed today to distinguish between two kinds of sciences: the *natural* or *physical* sciences, including physics, chemistry, and biology; and the *social* or *behavioral* sciences, including psychology, sociology, anthropology, economics, and political science. This way of distinguishing between them has its roots in the eighteenth century, when Newtonian mechanics was regarded as the model of a successful science. Since positive social research first began on a significant scale during this period, it was natural that its character would be affected by the Newtonian model. The idea of developing a comparable science of human nature or science of society captured the imaginations of thinking people. Would it be possible to apply Newton's "experimental method of reasoning," which had proved so successful in dealing with physical phenomena, to the explanation and prediction of human actions and social processes?

The social sciences have thus been conceived from the very beginning to be extensions of the natural sciences, and their history has been conditioned by men's determination to create a natural or experimental science of society.[1]

1

Today's conception of the task of the social sciences has evolved from this eighteenth-century origin and is, in brief, to provide us with empirically tested, systematic knowledge of human societies and their constituents. Human societies may be regarded as *aggregates* of individual human actions, together with their interrelations, interactions, and the consequences of such interactions, intended or unintended—for example, the formation of men into political and economic organizations. Alternatively, they may be regarded as *totalities* or *wholes,* with their own individuating properties, structures, or functional elements. These two ways of regarding human societies are not necessarily incompatible, although philosophers still dispute as to whether one view or the other is dispensable.[2] Psychologists and economists tend to study human societies as aggregates of individual actions, while sociologists and anthropologists prefer the alternate approach. Social scientists, whichever view they hold, seek explanations and predictions of human actions, and the way these actions are affected by human beings living in groups. They also seek knowledge of the history of social institutions, the principles of social cohesion and disruption, and the laws (if any) governing social and historical changes.

Philosophy has contributed to the history of the social sciences in two ways. First, philosophers have attempted to show, against various objections stemming from traditional theological or metaphysical sources, that the *idea* of a social science modelled on Newtonian methods is coherent and intelligible. David Hume (1711–1776), whose views will be examined at length in the next chapter, is an example of a philosopher who concerned himself with this kind of task. Second, they have tried to specify which of the various methods applied in the natural sciences could be adapted successfully to the study of human societies. This was the procedure adopted by John Stuart Mill (1806–1873) in his *A System of Logic,* Book VI, "On the Logic of the Moral Sciences" (1843), and has since been followed by most writers on the philosophy of social science.[3]

On the other hand, some writers have proceeded on the assumption that the social sciences must develop their own methods of inquiry independently of the methods of the natural sciences. From their point of view, the social sciences belong to a different *species* of science from the natural sciences. Hence, for them, the methods of explaining social phenomena must be different from the methods of explaining physical phenomena. Max Weber (1864–1920) is the best known exponent of this point of view. For Weber, the actual and possible achievements of the social sciences must not be measured by a yardstick borrowed from the natural sciences.[4]

We have here two opposed conceptions of the relation of social science to natural science. The outlook that predominates today derives from Hume and Mill; we shall call it *empiricism*. According to this view, the logic of concept formation, theory construction, and testing of hypotheses is the same in both natural and social sciences. Any differences that exist between the methods of the two kinds of science pertain to procedures for discovering or finding out relevant facts, rather than to methods of explaining or justifying descriptive or explanatory claims about the facts. For this reason, contemporary empiricists emphasize a distinction between *the context of discovery* and *the context of justification*. In the context of justification, but only in this context, they assert, there is a unity of method between natural and social sciences.[5] Thus, although there may be many interesting differences in the methods or techniques of research employed respectively in social and natural sciences, and in the types or characters of the subject matters of these sciences, these differences belong exclusively to the context of discovery (according to the empiricist). Indeed, similar kinds of differences in techniques of research and in types of subject matter may be found between various branches of natural science, such as physics, biology, geology, etc., but the logic of explaining events or justifying explanatory hypotheses is the same. Thus empiricists deny that the customary classification of sciences into natural and social has any important epistemological significance.

According to the second view, which we shall call *interpretationism,* the social sciences differ from the natural sciences with respect to the kinds of knowledge they produce. Hence to suppose that the social sciences can really progress or develop by emulating the methods of the natural sciences would be a mistake. The difference between social and natural science is comparable to that between natural science on the one hand, and mathematics and philosophy on the other. The natural sciences proceed by testing hypotheses on the basis of empirical observation of their predictive consequences. Their aim is to explain why things happen, in terms of a simple system of laws which are experimentally confirmed, and to predict future happenings. Mathematics, on the other hand, proceeds by deducing theorems from axioms or postulates, in accordance with laws of logic, and its results are independent of what is observed to happen in the course of nature. Thus, while the conclusions of natural science depend on observation and experience, the conclusions of mathematics are valid *a priori.*

Philosophy, according to the interpretationist, is like mathematics in that it is based on *a priori* reflection concerning relations of concepts. Unlike mathematics, however, its aim is not to prove theorems, nor to establish laws of number and the like, but to clarify and improve our understanding of reality, and the language we use to describe, explain, and evaluate our experience. Philosophy also differs from mathematics in that its method of reflection is not necessarily systematic, and its concepts are often vague.

From the interpretationist standpoint, the social sciences fall somewhere between natural science and philosophy.

Thus the social sciences involve many questions that are philosophical or quasi-philosophical in character, e.g., questions such as the conceptual differentiation of social phenomena from physical phenomena, the relation of people's beliefs to their actions, whether a society is identical to the collective actions of the individuals composing it or is something independent of the particular individuals and their actions, and so on. Furthermore, when a social scientist investigates a particular social organization, he has to understand the religious, moral, and metaphysical views of the members of that organization, and how those views affect their actions and help to determine the character of their social institutions. For these and similar reasons, the interpretationist concludes that much of the essential work of the social scientist resembles more the task of the philosopher than that of the physicist; for much of his work consists of *a priori* reflection on the relations of concepts held by members of the society under study. Thus, "observations" of the social structure of an alien society would be of little value unless they were accompanied by an understanding of that structure from the point of view of the members of that society, rather than from the cultural standpoint of the scientific observer.

This claim—that it is essential to interpret people's conceptualizations or their understanding of reality if one wants to understand their society—is the reason this position is called *interpretationism*. An interpretationist is therefore one who believes that in studying human behavior or social practices and institutions, we must take account of the inner or subjective view of the persons or societies under study, if our conclusions are to have genuine explanatory value. The interpretationist also argues that this characteristic of social studies is unique, that there is nothing quite like it in the natural sciences, and that it implies that there are differences between the social and natural sciences in the nature and force of explanation and the methods of justifying hypotheses. Thus the interpretationist rejects the empiricist's distinction between the context of discovery and the context of justification, at least so far as this distinction is supposed to support the unity of method thesis.[6]

A Glance Ahead.

The reader may find a brief account of the road we shall travel helpful.

The second chapter introduces basic principles of empiricism by means of a detailed critical examination of David Hume's *science of human nature.* Hume tried to show that we could explain psychological and social phenomena by the same principles used in the natural sciences to explain physical events and processes. Hume is thus one of the earliest advocates of the unity of method thesis described above. This thesis characterizes *empiricism* in the philosophy of the social sciences, just as its denial characterizes *interpretationism.*

Hume, however, failed to arrive at a consistent theory of knowledge which could support his thesis of the unity of method. Hume presupposed a distinction between the way each of us knows his own "ideas," which include his conscious motives, desires, and beliefs, and the way we may know the events and processes of the "external world." According to Hume, the former kind of knowledge is immediate, certain, and beyond the possibility of verification by scientific methods. Our knowledge of the external world, on the other hand, concerns intersubjectively observable events and processes. It is not immediate but "experimental," not certain but only "probable." Thus these two kinds of knowledge, for Hume, have incompatible properties. At the same time, societal knowledge, so far as it concerns people's motives, desires, and beliefs, depends on the kind of knowledge we have of our own immediate experiences. Since the latter kind of knowledge necessarily falls outside the bounds of scientific inquiry, it appears to follow that societal knowledge, in its foundations, must also be beyond the reach of science. Consequently, Hume was unable to establish his thesis that the "experimental method of reasoning" of the natural sciences could be applied systematically to the study of psychological or social phenomena.

Discussion of Hume's version of empiricism sets the stage for the introduction of interpretationism in the third chapter, in connection with the methodological views of Max Weber. Weber's notions are contrasted with Émile Durkheim's, which represent an important development in nineteenth-century empiricism. Hegel, Marx, and J. S. Mill are also briefly reviewed in this chapter, by way of an introduction to developments in nineteenth-century thought.

I discuss the conflict between Weber and Durkheim in the following terms. Social events, unlike events studied in natural science, consist in actions of people who have their own ideas about what they are doing or why they are doing it. These ideas include their beliefs, which may be true or false, as well as their reasons for acting. Must the social scientist, in attempting to describe or explain social events, refer to or perhaps even use those people's own ideas about their behavior in framing *his* explanations? Durkheim denied this, and asserted that the social scientist could explain social phenomena by reference to "causes unperceived by consciousness." Weber, on the other hand, asserted that we can explain large-scale social developments, such as the emergence of capitalistic economic institutions between the sixteenth and nineteenth centuries, only if we can first understand the motives, beliefs, and goals of the individual human agents who caused them.

However, Weber and Durkheim agreed on one important point: that *if* people's ideas must be used to explain their behavior or to understand social events, then social studies must have an entirely different character from natural science. For Durkheim, accepting this hypothesis was tantamount to denying the possibility of achieving scientific knowledge of social uniformities and changes. For

Weber, accepting it was necessary for a proper understanding of the purposes of sociological inquiry and explanation. The conflict between these two conceptions of the aims of social inquiry and the kind of knowledge it can achieve, emerges as the principal issue of this book and perhaps of the epistemology of the social sciences.

I try to show that the conflict in Durkheim's and Weber's views arose in part from Hume's unsolved epistemological problem, described above. Weber emphasized the importance of first-person or subjective psychological concepts for our understanding of social phenomena, while Durkheim emphasized the importance of technical, theoretical concepts for constructing a genuinely experimental social science. By eliminating all reference to *consciousness* from the scope of social science, Durkheim made an important advance beyond Hume, from the standpoint of empiricism.

Consideration of Durkheim's thesis raises the question whether a social science of the sort he envisions is really intelligible or possible. According to Peter Winch, a contemporary philosopher whose views are examined in chapter IV, a social science which did not utilize the "ideas of participants" in framing its explanations would be logically impossible, a contradiction in terms. Winch also argues that social studies which do make use of participant ideas cannot be purely experimental and must employ resources of *verstehen* as indicated by Max Weber.[7] The thesis that Winch fails to establish satisfactorily is that any social science *must* make use of participant ideas. But this thesis is necessary in order to derive the conclusion that a Durkheimian form of social science is logically impossible. We cannot preclude the possibility of a social science which explains and predicts social events in terms foreign to the ideas and language of participants in the social process.

Winch's thesis raises the question whether causal explanations, in Hume's sense (see chapter II), can be applied to human actions. Chapter V reviews this question, and considers whether there is a non-causal kind of explanation that can be applied to human actions. The view that causal explanations of human actions are impossible seems to arise from a confusion of the action itself with some standard way of describing or talking about the action. Just as there can be different kinds of descriptions of the same event, so there can be different kinds of explanations of the same event under these different kinds of descriptions. I argue that there is an important kind of explanation used in social science and everyday life, which is not causal but "interpretive," and that nothing is gained by attempting to reduce interpretive explanations to strictly causal form. I also argue that we can apply both interpretive and causal types of explanations to human actions, but often the former is available when the latter is not. I connect this thesis with Weber's methodological views, thereby suggesting that interpretationism can be defended as a viable form of social science. We can go even further and say that when there is no alternative to using the language or ideas of participants in framing our explanations of their actions, interpretationism is correct and empiricism incorrect in their respective accounts of the nature of social science. Thus in the end my account agrees with Peter Winch's, with the important qualification that my view does not imply the *logical* impossibility of a strictly empiricistic social science.

Earlier we saw that so far as the social sciences employ concepts derived from our experience of ourselves as conscious beings, they cannot at the same time use experimental methods of verifying statements containing those concepts. This gives rise to the question whether social sciences *must* utilize concepts of this type. The last three chapters are devoted to a discussion of various aspects of this problem. In chapter VI, *logical behaviorism* is explained as an attempt to show that the language of psychology, linguistics, and related disciplines can be divested of all subjective psychological or "mentalistic" concepts, and of all forms of discourse implying a relation between a person's psychological state and the "objects" apparently contained in that state. Clearly, if logical behaviorism could be made to work, this would be an important boost for empiricism. Consideration of logical behaviorism raises many problems in semantic analysis, some of which are discussed in this chapter.

The converse thesis of the indispensability of mentalistic terms for describing or explaining certain human states or dispositions is considered in chapter VII, under the heading of "the problem of intentionality." I attempt to show that just as the logical behaviorists were unable to prove their thesis that the language of social science can be divested of mentalistic terms, so "intentionalists" are unable to prove that this *cannot* be done. I then suggest a new view of the whole problem, namely that the presence of mentalistic terms in the language of science, or the grammatical constructions to which the use of such terms gives rise, is compatible with a scientific orientation provided we expand our conception of "science" beyond the characteristic empiricist conception deriving from Hume and Durkheim. This involves the consideration, originally advanced by Rudolf Carnap, that mentalistic terms and sentences could occur in theories which as a *whole* are empirically testable, in the sense that such theories could yield predictions testable by the orthodox methods of science.

But this step brings us squarely into conflict with W.V.O. Quine's thesis of *translational indeterminacy,* which is examined in chapter VIII. Quine's view seems to be that certain higher-order "translational hypotheses" concerning identity of meaning between sentences belonging to culturally divergent languages, are incapable of empirical test, since they do not express any "objective fact." Consequently, the occurrence of such hypotheses in a scientific theory which is testable as a whole, would be meaningless, since they could not possibly add anything to the theory in question. If Quine is right, then questions typically raised by interpretationists would necessarily fall outside the scope of science since these questions often involve comparing and contrasting "the meaning" of certain human actions occurring in culturally divergent social systems.

I try to show that Quine's argument for translational indeterminacy is not a compelling one, and besides, that the thesis has certain paradoxical consequences. I also suggest a means of treating questions of identity of meaning across different languages as questions of objective fact, although this involves adopting a form of semantic analysis that Quine would reject. I conclude that social sciences need not confine themselves to strictly behavioristic methods of inquiry; moreover, it appears that they would suffer in scope and explanatory power if they attempted to do so.

II

David Hume's
Science of Human Nature

The Method of Inquiry.

We said above that philosophical interest in the possibility of an experimental social science goes back at least as far as the eighteenth century, to the debate about a science of human nature or a science of society which would emulate the methods of Newtonian physics and perhaps achieve a similar success. David Hume's philosophical work is an excellent example of this eighteenth-century approach to the theory of the social sciences. Unlike many of his contemporaries and successors, however, Hume did not merely speculate concerning the possibility of such a science; he set out to construct the main principles of a science of human nature, including a method for making "discoveries" in that science, which he applied and illustrated by "results" in the course of the three volumes of his *A Treatise of Human Nature* (1739–40).[1] Along the way he worked out a theory of "experimental reasoning" and provided an analysis of the relation of cause and effect which is still at the forefront of philosophical discussion.

Unfortunately, the significance of Hume's *Treatise* escaped the attention of the learned world of his time, and Hume himself later came to regard his early ambitions to found a science of man as ill-advised. History has since re-versed the verdict of Hume and his contemporaries regard-ing the value of the *Treatise*. This work is now viewed as one of the most important philosophical books of all time, and as genuinely revolutionary for our understanding of both philosophy and the sciences. Even so, the relevance of Hume's work to the epistemology of the social sciences is still not widely appreciated. This lack of appreciation is due in part to a failure to study the *Treatise* systematically and as a whole, and in part to a failure to take seriously Hume's claim to have worked out a *method* for making discoveries in the field of psychological or social science.

Hume's *Treatise* was explicitly subtitled: "Being an At-tempt to Introduce the Experimental Method of Reason-ing into Moral Subjects." The term *moral subjects* meant to Hume, as it did to other philosophers of the Enlighten-ment, any subject involving human nature or activity—especially human conduct, social practices, and the feelings, emotions, and thoughts of individual men. A *moral science* was any rational inquiry into such matters, or any matter knowledge of which would have a direct and important bearing on men's conduct of life. Thus the term *moral science* designated not only all the sciences that we today call social and psychological, but also such diverse subjects as natural religion, aesthetics, criticism; and inquiries such as ethics or epistemology that we classify as philosophical.

Perhaps the principal defect in Hume's conception of the experimental method is the lack of any procedure for determining whether the *results* of his *experiments* ex-tended beyond his own case. Nor did he distinguish between what we might call psychological laws, i.e., state-ments true of humanity in general, and sociological gen-eralizations which may have been true of people of Hume's own cultural background and education, but did not neces-sarily extend to human beings belonging to different cultural backgrounds. But if Hume's method was incapable of establishing results of the kind of universality we seek in science, the fact that he was among the first to see the need for constructing a specific method of inquiry in the social sciences insures his historical importance. For his perception of this need led him to study many of the important epistemological problems that constitute stumbling blocks to the progress of the social sciences, and it is his work on these problems that continues to have contemporary relevance. Since understanding Hume's theory of knowledge is essential for understanding central problems of the philosophy of social science, we shall have to devote considerable space to an exposition and criticism of his basic doctrines.

The Primacy of the Moral Sciences.

If we assume that a society is an organization of men which only exists in and through individuals and their actions, then there can be a science of society, or of men as united in groups by customs, laws, and shared practices, only if a science of individual human actions is possible. This was clearly recognized by Hume, who saw that if an empirical social science was to be achieved, then *the same kinds of relations* must hold between human actions and their causes, as held between the motions of bodies and their causes. Only if this were true, Hume thought, could we apply the same methods of knowledge in both social and natural sciences.

According to Hume, the content of the science of human nature would consist of the conclusions which resulted from applying the experimental method of reasoning to moral subjects. In Hume's time, more so than in our own day, most philosophers would have considered it doubtful, if not absurd, to suppose that the experimental method could fruitfully be applied to the study of human activities. Hence there was a task which Hume had to accomplish before social or moral science itself could come into existence. This was the *epistemological* one of showing that it was indeed possible (i.e., logically consistent and coherent) to apply the experimental method to moral subjects. Hume thought it was sufficient, in order to show this (1) to explain the real nature of the experimental method of reasoning as applied to natural phenomena, and (2) to show that the same relations of phenomena found in natural subjects are also found in moral ones.

In the Introduction to the *Treatise* Hume discusses the relation of the sciences. All the "sciences," he there reasons, i.e., all the departments of human knowledge or inquiry, "lie under the cognizance of men, and are judged of by their powers or faculties." The achievement of certainty or truth in any field of inquiry is therefore dependent in part on the capability and reliability of our cognitive faculties, or our power to know anything. It follows that the sciences are incomplete as long as we remain without any reliable information about men's powers or faculties of judgment. It is the business of the science of man to provide us with this kind of information, by acquainting us with "the extent and force of human understanding," and by explaining "the nature of the ideas we employ, and of the operations we perform in our reasonings." In this way, every science can be seen to be "in some measure dependent on the science of man," including sciences apparently as remote from any connection with human nature as mathematics, physics (i.e., "natural philosophy"), and "natural religion" (p. ix).

Hume's point here is twofold. On the one hand, a field of inquiry which is not concerned with man, such as mathematics and physics, is feasible only if human faculties of conception and judgment can conceivably arrive at truth or knowledge in that field. On the other hand, a field of inquiry such as *natural religion*—which deals with the natural or empirical, as opposed to revealed, grounds for believing in the existence of God—has *implications* for human life and conduct. So even in the case of inquiries apparently remote from human nature, the latter is nevertheless implicated in them, either as cause or consequence. And in the moral or social sciences, "we ourselves are not only the beings, that reason, but also one of the objects, concerning which we reason." Among the moral sciences that Hume enumerates are *logic, morals and criticism,* and *politics.*

Hume's use of these terms is considerably different from that which prevails today. Logic, for Hume, includes what we distinguish as formal or symbolic logic, epistemology, or the theory of knowledge, and the psychology of belief. *Morals and criticism* would include ethics or moral philosophy, aesthetics, and the psychology of attitudes and sensations; *politics* would include the various branches of social science (e.g., economics, sociology, etc.) as well as social and political philosophy. Thus Hume does not presuppose the same kinds of distinctions that are made today between a *philosophical* and a *scientific* question about human faculties. Nowadays, for instance, the term *logic* would signify the study of rules of *valid* reasoning or inference, as opposed to a study of "the operations we perform in our reasonings." The latter would be classified as belonging to empirical psychology, i.e., to the empirical study of how people do reason, regardless of whether their reasoning is valid or invalid, correct or incorrect. On the other hand, the rules of validity studied in formal or inductive logic are commonly regarded today as in no way dependent on whether people's reasoning conforms to them, or whether, for that matter, people reason at all. Similarly for the other subjects that Hume mentions. *Morals and criticism,* so far as they concern the criteria or standards for correct judgment, would belong to moral philosophy and aesthetics; so far as they concern the way people actually do make moral and aesthetic judgments, they would belong to psychology. Finally, we tend to think of the political and social sciences as being concerned with people's actual behavior, their motives, the causes of their behavior, the actual structure of their societies, and their real political and social aims, with all the conflict and diversity that these activities exhibit to observation. Social and political philosophy, on the other hand, study such questions as what forms of political constitution men *ought* to seek, or what forms of social organization are *desirable* for men.

Since Hume does not presuppose any such systematic distinction between the scientific and the philosophical aspects of these subjects, his conception of the "science of man" may be said to be *normative* and *epistemological.* His aim is not merely to describe and explain the causes and conditions of why people believe, reason, judge, or behave as they do; but also *why what they believe is sometimes true; why their reasoning is sometimes valid or productive of genuine knowledge, why their moral or aesthetic judgments are sometimes correct,* and so on. But Hume is not uncritically or unthinkingly confusing psychological considerations with logical and normative ones, as is sometimes urged; on the contrary, he is proposing to show how we can apply the experimental method to solve such logical and normative problems as whether *knowledge* is possible for men, the nature of the human good, the right and wrong in human conduct, and so on. From Hume's point of view, to separate the normative and descriptive aspect of these studies and utterly divorce the former from the latter would be to trivialize "the science of man," or to transform it from a *science* on which all other sciences are dependent into one which is dependent on them. The present day tendency to view the psychological and social sciences as dependent on the sciences of physics and biology is therefore exactly the *reverse* of Hume's thinking about the relation of these sciences.

The correctness of this interpretation of Hume is borne out by passages such as the following from the *Treatise:*

> There is no question of importance, whose decision is not compriz'd in the science of man; and there is none, which can be decided with any certainty, before we become acquainted with that science.... In pretending therefore to

> explain the principles of human nature, we in effect pro-
> pose a compleat system of the sciences, built on a founda-
> tion almost entirely new, and the only one upon which
> they can stand with any security (p. xx).

Hume, then, is conscious of the revolutionary character of
his project; his aim is to achieve nothing less than an empirical science of the *a priori* conditions of all the sciences
of nature and *morals* (including natural religion).

But the science of man, as the science of the *a priori* conditions of all the other sciences, is not itself *a priori* but
empirical: ". . . as the science of man is the only solid
foundation for the other sciences, so the only solid foundation we can give to this science itself must be laid on experience and observation" (*ibid.*).

To have *a priori* knowledge of human nature would be
to know, independently of all experience and observation,
the causes of human behavior or what particular effects
those causes will have in different circumstances and situations. According to Hume, we could only have this kind of
knowledge of human nature if we were acquainted with the
"essence" of the human mind. For we could then *deduce,*
prior to any actual observations, how the mind would act
in given circumstances. But in fact, Hume claims, we cannot possibly have any such knowledge of "essences":

> . . . to me it seems evident, that the essence of the mind
> being equally unknown to us with that of external bodies,
> it must be equally impossible to form any notion of its
> powers and qualities otherwise than from careful and exact
> experiments, and the observation of those particular ef-
> fects, which result from its different circumstances and situ-
> ations (p. xxi).

Since human faculties do not extend to the knowledge
of essences, including our own, all of our knowledge of
human faculties must be observational and experimental.
If the aim of the science of man were "the explaining of
the ultimate principles of the soul," then such a science
would be impossible. But what experience teaches us, in

this science, is to limit our ambitions to what can be established on the basis of experience. The experimental method can lead us to certain "general principles," which, though we must endeavor to render them as universal as possible, we cannot honestly pretend to explain further. Nor are these principles intelligible in themselves, or evident to reason. Our only reason for believing them, Hume thinks, is "our experience of their reality." If this is a sceptical doctrine, then Hume believes that scepticism is part and parcel of scientific method. For no science of existence "can go beyond experience, or establish any principles which are not founded on that authority" (p. xxii). Thus *moral* and natural sciences are alike in that they are limited to what can be known by experience.

Hume mentions only one respect in which the sciences of man are restricted in comparison with the natural sciences: we cannot practice artificial or controlled experiments on ourselves as subjects, since our consciousness of the fact that we are experimenting on ourselves would introduce a new causative factor into the situation and thereby invalidate the experiment. "We must therefore glean up our experiments in this science," Hume says, "from a cautious observation of human life, and take them as they appear in the common course of the world, by men's behaviour in company, in affairs, and in their pleasures" (p. xxiii). The data of the moral sciences must be gathered from history and from observation of men's social practices. This limitation, however, is not destructive of the possibility of achieving scientific knowledge of human nature, since when "experiments of this kind are judiciously collected and compared, we may hope to establish on them a science, which will not be inferior in certainty . . . to any other of human comprehension" (*Ibid.*).

Hume here touches on a methodological problem of science which he fails to develop properly. On the one hand, his argument that artificial or controlled experiment is impossible in moral science presupposes that the data of such a science must be internal or psychological, and therefore capable of being observed directly by one person only, namely the person whose experiences form the data. It is only because we cannot experiment artificially with our own experiences without thereby altering them, that he concludes that artificial experiments are impossible in moral science. He then points to "men's behaviour" as the arena from which we can "glean up our experiments in this science." Hume does not seem to notice that men's *behavior* is external and open to public observation, unlike the data of consciousness; nor does he consider the possibility of contriving artificial experiments involving behavior, as opposed to data of consciousness. But if we can use men's behavior in history and society as a basis for inferring general conclusions, there is no reason why we could not artificially experiment with their behavior in order to test those conclusions. Such experiments need not alter the character of the behavior, so long as the experimental subjects do not suspect the aim or hypothesis of the experiment.

Aspects of Knowledge.

There is, however, a more serious philosophical perplexity which arises in connection with Hume's conception of the sciences of man. As we have seen, the aim of these sciences, as Hume characterizes it, is not merely to describe, explain, or predict human behavior; it is also to explain why what men believe is sometimes true, or how they may arrive at knowledge, why their moral judgments are sometimes correct, and so on. But the fact that a person is *caused* to believe something, for example, does not imply that his belief is true, although a good and sufficient reason for believing something may also cause one to believe it. Similarly, the fact that someone is *caused* to make a certain moral judgment does not imply that his judgment is morally correct or obligatory. In general, then, a science of *behavior,* and a "science" of the criteria of validity of warranted beliefs, or a science of *customs* and *mores* and a "science" of criteria of correct moral judgments, seem to be quite different subjects. Yet Hume seems to lump them together.

Hume would justify this procedure by pointing out that human knowledge, including science, does not exist in a void; it is a mode of *human* reason or understanding, i.e., a relation between men, with their specific and finite capacities, and those objects which fall within the range of their cognizance. The word *knowledge* and its synonyms, in other words, are *relational* predicates. A sentence involving the term *knowledge* requires at least two terms, a knower and a known.

It follows that every claim to human knowledge may be analyzed from two aspects: a *subjective* aspect, relating to the knower, and an *objective* aspect, relating to the known. In any science, assumptions about the subjective aspect of knowledge are no less essential and unavoidable than assumptions about the objective aspect. For example, the customary distinction between what we can know by *observation* and what we can know, if at all, only by *inference* from what we can observe, is a distinction that relates to human faculties and the powers and limits of human organs of observation. Yet this distinction is important for understanding science; for instance, in determining suitable *observational* conditions for testing a hypothesis. Nevertheless, the various natural sciences do not try to make their assumptions about the subjective conditions of knowledge explicit, nor do they treat these assumptions as part of the science. This is partly because the *same* assumptions about the subjective aspect of knowledge are common to every natural science. It is only by their *objective* assumptions that the different natural sciences can be distinguished. For example, Newton's laws of motion constitute a set of objective postulates or assumptions, and these laws determine for us the field of investigation of Newtonian mechanics. Chemistry, biology, etc., would be similarly distinguished by what they set out as their respective objective assumptions concerning the fields they propose to investigate.

Assumptions concerning the nature of the objects of knowledge are such that they can conceivably be replaced or corrected in the ordinary course of experience and scientific investigation. That is to say, as we learn more about the objects we are investigating and their relations, we can correct our *ideas* and *beliefs* about them. Experience may teach us that water, when it freezes, will expand, while other familiar liquids will contract when they freeze. In this way, our *conceptions* or *ideas* of liquids may undergo a change.

The question is whether assumptions about the *subjective* aspect of knowledge—e.g., about the nature of *concepts* or *ideas*—can be corrected by experience in the same way. At the beginning of the eighteenth century, philosophers assumed that questions about the power of the human mind to form ideas, or about the scope and limits of human knowledge, were *subjective* in character, i.e., they concerned human faculties of knowledge; and that the correct answers to these questions determined the range of *possible* objects of empirical inquiry or knowledge. Hence the question arose, what sorts of ideas are possible for the human mind?

It appeared that this question could not be answered in the ordinary course of a scientific investigation, since the latter can only disclose what is in fact the case within the range of what is possibly the case, i.e., within the range of what the human mind can conceive. If so, the results of empirical or scientific inquiry cannot bear logically on, nor therefore tend to be corrective of, assumptions about the power of the human mind to form ideas, since *these* assumptions determine the limits of what we can *conceive* or possibly know.

Now if every department of human inquiry involves assumptions of both the objective and subjective kinds, then moral or social sciences are no exception. Here, however, a complication arises, due to the fact that in the moral or social sciences not only the *subject* but also the *object* of knowledge is man, in his cultural and mental manifestations and activities. Thus, unlike the physical or natural sciences, in the social sciences assumptions about the nature of the *objects* of inquiry are also assumptions about the nature of the *inquirers*—the *subjects* of knowledge. In addition, the human activities investigated by the moral sciences include systems of philosophy, religion, language, the production of ideas, and science itself—any of which may enter into the course of history and help to determine the character of a society and the social relations which are dominant at a particular time. But systems of philosophy, religion, etc., include their *own* assumptions about the subjective aspects of knowledge—assumptions which are *a priori* in relation to the empirical facts and help to determine what are conceived to be the scope and limits of human knowledge. Thus it appears that a *moral science* cannot be on a par with a natural science, for the *objective* assumptions which are necessary to moral inquiry constitute, in effect, a rival system of philosophy *vis-à-vis* the systems of human ideas or conduct which it proposes to investigate. In other words, the moral scientist is in a position analogous to that of the philosopher confronting a rival system of philosophy, rather than a position analogous to that of a natural scientist investigating some aspect of the physical universe.

Two problems therefore confronted Hume when he set out to construct an empirical science of human nature. The first was the problem of how to determine the scope and limits of human knowledge without begging the fundamental question of epistemology—namely, which set of assumptions concerning the power of the human mind to form ideas is correct or true. The second problem was how to show that "moral phenomena" could be profitably investigated by scientific methods.

Hume proposed to deal with the first problem as follows. He introduced the term *perception* to stand for whatever the human mind can conceive, imagine, or experience. Hence all ideas were perceptions, as well as all images, passions, sensations, etc. Hume then claimed that we experience some of these perceptions as simple or unanalyzable, and others as complex or analyzable. Furthermore, some of the complex perceptions, Hume thought, were evidently made up of simple ones. Thus our idea of an apple consisted of a combination of simple ideas of color, shape, etc. Hume thought that all this was obvious to introspection. He then generalized this observation and arrived at the principle that in order to determine whether any doubtful proposition went beyond the possible scope of human knowledge, e.g., "the soul is immortal," "God answers sincere prayers," and so on, we had to examine the "ideas of which it was composed." The idea of a "soul," for example, if it was a genuine or meaningful idea, must be derivable from some set of simple perceptions. By this method, Hume thought we could have an empirical test to determine whether any proposed hypothesis fell within or exceeded the limits of possible human knowledge. If we could not discover the simple perceptions from which the ideas in the hypothesis were supposedly derived, then the hypothesis was probably beyond the scope of human knowledge. In this way we could deal with rival philosophical or religious systems. If their hypotheses were determined to fall outside the scope of human knowledge, they could be dismissed as meaningless. If these hypotheses fell within the scope of possible human knowledge, then they could be tested empirically, by scientific methods of reasoning.

Hume's method of determining the meaningfulness and hence the empirical testability of a claim to knowledge or belief is ingenious, but its validity is questionable. Apart from the unproved assumption that our experience can be broken down into simple, unanalyzable perceptions, Hume offers no effective procedure for determining whether the method of deriving complex ideas from simple ones is correctly applied in a given instance. He therefore has no way of distinguishing between merely an incorrect application of the method, and a case in which an alleged complex idea is meaningless because it really does not consist of any simple ones. Thus Hume does not really solve the problem of how a moral science can be on a par with natural sciences; for Hume's *moral science* really is a philosophical system, competing with other, rival philosophical systems which make very different assumptions concerning human powers of conception, and of the scope and limits of human knowledge.

Hume attempted to resolve the second problem—the problem of showing how *moral phenomena* could be investigated by scientific methods, in the following way. He argued that human actions, including conscious or intentional ones, were "caused" by men's motives, circumstances, and temperament, in the sense that there is a "constant conjunction" of types of motives with types of actions. He also held that this same relation of constant conjunction was the foundation of our causal knowledge of the natural world. In order to understand this doctrine correctly, and to appreciate its strong and weak points, we shall have to review some of the details of Hume's analysis of our idea of causality, as well as his criticism of the traditional doctrine of causality. We shall also have to examine his theory of the nature of our knowledge of causal relations, and of how we may know and explain human actions. An important part of Hume's theory was his denial of logical or necessary connections of events or existing things, i.e., connections that might be known *a priori* or independently of observation and experience.

The experimental method of reasoning of natural science, Hume argued, is nothing but "causal inference," which depended for its validity on there being an appropriate relation of causality or constant conjunction between the kinds of objects being reasoned about. Having shown, as he believed, that there is such a relation of constant conjunction between the motives of human actions and the actions themselves, Hume inferred that human actions were caused in the same sense as the events of physics, and therefore that the same method of reasoning which was employed by the latter could be applied to the study of human actions.

Hume's philosophy of the moral or social sciences may be regarded as the first systematic presentation and defense of the unity of method thesis mentioned in the previous chapter, i.e., the theory that the same methods of inquiry are employed in both the social and the natural sciences. As we shall see, Hume's attempt to provide a systematic defense of this thesis collapses from internal stresses arising from two main sources. On the one hand, he is unable to reconcile his view of all empirical knowledge as experimental and fallible, with his view that each person's knowledge of his own conscious experiences is immediate and infallible. On the other hand, Hume is unable to solve a central problem in epistemology, namely, how knowledge of the minds of other people is possible. Since these problems arise from Hume's conception of the experimental method of reasoning, we shall have to discuss this latter topic first.

Hume's Experimental Method of Reasoning.

For Hume, our "understanding" or cognitive faculty consists of the faculties of sensation, memory, introspection or consciousness, and reason. The materials of knowledge are "impressions" or "original perceptions," and their residues left in the mind after their first appearance, which Hume calls "ideas." Ideas are thus multiply related to impressions—on the one hand, the former are "copies" or replicas of the latter; on the other hand, they are caused by impressions. Considered as copies, the relation between ideas and their impressions is a *meaning relation,* i.e., the

ideas "stand for" or "denote" the impressions. Hume sometimes speaks of impressions as if they were *identical* with
the physical objects that we perceive, and at other times
he speaks of them as if they were sensations which are
presumably *caused* by the physical objects. In either case,
ideas are materials of knowledge only so far as they are
copies of impressions. Knowledge is having true ideas, but
not merely that, since we may have true ideas without having knowledge. According to Hume, "truth is discern'd
merely by ideas, and by their juxta-position and comparison." Reason is the faculty whereby we discover truth or
falsehood, and the latter consist in "an agreement or disagreement either to the *real* relations of ideas, or to *real*
existence and matter of fact" (III.1.i). The possibility of
falsehood arises from the fact that ideas may be combined
in a way that does not agree with some real relation of
ideas, or some real existence and matter of fact.

A central principle in Hume's epistemology is the distinction between *reasoning* and *perceiving*.

> All kinds of reasoning consist in nothing but a comparison,
> and a discovery of those relations, either constant or in-
> constant, which two or more objects bear to each other
> (I.3.ii).

Hume considers three possibilities: (i) both objects are
present to the senses, (ii) neither object is present, and
(iii) only one is present. "When both objects are present to
the senses along with the relation," Hume says, "we call
this perception rather than reasoning. . ." (*ibid.*). Thus
reasoning, properly speaking, occurs only when there is a
discovery or comparison of objects or their relations, and
not all the objects and their relations are present to the
senses (or memory), i.e., the objects or relations implicated
in the discovery or comparison. Perception, on the other
hand, is "a mere passive admission of impressions thro' the
organs of sensation" (*ibid.*). According to Hume *perception* involves no "exercise of the thought, or any action,

properly speaking" (*ibid.*). Hume suggests, then, that reasoning or thought, as contrasted with perception, is an *activity*. Since perception does not "go beyond what is immediately present to the senses" (or memory), reasoning is necessary in order "to discover the real existence of the relations of objects" (*ibid.*). By *real existence* in this context Hume means existence of objects independent of the senses or memory. Thus, for Hume, neither memory nor sensation by itself enables us to discover "the real existence of the relations of objects."

All relations, in the sense of "any particular subject of comparison," may be divided into two classes; "into such as depend entirely on the ideas, which we compare together, and such as may be chang'd without any change in the ideas" (I.3.i). This division of relations into two classes is of fundamental importance to Hume's theory of knowledge. The implications of this distinction are brought out by Hume as follows:

> 'Tis from the idea of a triangle, that we discover the relation of equality, which its three angles bear to two right ones; and this relation is invariable, as long as our idea remains the same (*ibid.*).

In other words, we can discover or come to know, merely by examining our ideas, that the sum of the interior angles of a triangle is equal to two right ones. This relation of equality is therefore one that requires *nothing but* ideas in order to be discovered by the mind. When Hume goes on to say that "this relation is invariable as long as our idea remains the same," he means that the truth of the proposition:

> The sum of the three interior angles of a triangle is equal to the sum of two right angles,

depends on nothing more than these ideas being what they are. This type of relation has been called *internal* to the ideas related, since it is impossible to conceive of any change in this type of relation which does not imply a change in the ideas related. In other words, we cannot conceive or form the idea of a triangle the sum of whose interior angles is *not* equal to two right ones. Hence the above proposition is necessarily true and knowable *a priori*. Hume thinks that all mathematical and geometrical knowledge is of this type, i.e., it concerns internal relations of ideas and is therefore *a priori*.

On the other hand:

> ... the relations of *contiguity* and *distance* betwixt two objects may be chang'd merely by an alteration of their place, without any change on the objects themselves or on their ideas; and the place depends on a hundred different accidents, which cannot be foreseen by the mind (*ibid*.).

Thus, while we cannot "disturb" the relation of equality which holds between the three angles of a triangle and two right ones so long as our ideas of these things remain the same, we *can* imagine changes in relations such as *contiguity* or *distance* without disturbing or altering our ideas of the objects so related. For example, we can imagine two carts being brought closer together or moved farther apart. Relations of this kind have been called *external* because they do not necessarily remain invariable so long as "our ideas remain the same." Hence, our knowledge of any invariableness that exists in things externally related depends on *something more* than merely whether our ideas remain the same, i.e., on something more than merely the ideas. This "something more" is experience or observation.

For this reason, propositions concerning external relations alone are neither necessarily true nor knowable *a priori*. Now as we noted above, according to Hume we cannot perceive any relations which enable us to go beyond "what is immediately present to the senses or memory," in order to discover "the real existence of the relations of objects" independent of the mind. The only relation that enables us to make such an inference is *causality:*

> 'Tis only *causation*, which produces such a connexion, as
> to give us assurance from the existence or action of one
> object, that 'twas follow'd or preceded by any other exist-
> ence or action. . . (I.3.ii).

Thus in order to know anything of the existence or relations of things not present to the senses or memory, we must
employ reasoning whose validity or reliability depends on
the existence of a causal relation between the things we can
observe and the things not being observed. It is this kind
of reasoning that Hume calls "experimental"—namely
causal inference. Since causality is an external relation,
causal propositions are contingently true or false, and they
are knowable only *a posteriori* or on the basis of observation
and experience.

For Hume, then, all scientific knowledge is of relations,
but relations are of two kinds, namely (1) those which we
can discover merely by examining our ideas, and (2) those
for which we need experience and observation in order to
discover.[2] Relations of the former kind can be known *a
priori,* while those of the latter kind can only be known
a posteriori. Hence there are two, but only two, kinds of
scientific knowledge or inquiry: (1) *a priori* sciences,
and (2) *a posteriori* ones. All mathematical sciences are of
the former kind, while natural and moral sciences are of the
latter kind. Since all *a priori* knowledge (the only kind of
knowledge that can be certain) is of internal relations, and
hence does not go beyond the mere ideas, in order to know
anything about the real existence and relations of things
outside our ideas, we must obtain knowledge of causal
relations. Even judgments of the invariableness or identity
of objects in time depend on causation. But causal relations
are external and hence cannot be known with certainty.
Since our knowledge of causal relations depends on experience and observation, and since the natural sciences are
concerned with causal relations, it follows that the natural
sciences do not give us certainty in knowledge. At best they

give us what Hume calls "probability." Hume sums up his doctrine in the following passage:

> . . . There is no object, which implies the existence of any other if we consider these objects in themselves, and never look beyond the ideas which we form of them. Such an inference wou'd amount to knowledge, and wou'd imply the absolute contradiction and impossibility of conceiving any thing different. But as all distinct ideas are separable, 'tis evident there can be no impossibility of that kind. . . .
> 'Tis therefore by Experience only, that we can infer the existence of one object from that of another. . . (I.3.vi).

Hume's Analysis of Causality.

Hume's next step is to analyze the idea of causality. The essential propositions of his analysis are as follows:

(1) Causation is a relation and not a sensible quality of objects.

(2) It is a complex idea of relation, consisting of simpler ideas of relation. That is, "in considering any single instance of cause and effect" we find that we can observe nothing more than "the two relations of *contiguity* and *succession*." However,

> Contiguity and succession are not sufficient to make us pronounce any two objects to be cause and effect, unless we perceive, that these two relations are preserv'd in several instances (I.3.vi).

Hume refers to this conclusion as the discovery of "a new relation betwixt cause and effect. . . ." He calls this relation "their constant conjunction." Constant conjunction

> implies no more than this, that like objects have always been plac'd in like relations of contiguity and succession (*ibid.*) .

Hence,

(3) The causal relation is a relation between *classes* of events rather than between individual events, and every

true causal judgment implies a causal law (uniformity).[3]

What Hume tried to show is that the idea of causality is derived neither from individuating sensible qualities of objects nor from any internal relations of ideas. Yet there is something more to the idea of causality than merely the relations of contiguity and succession which we can observe. This additional condition is that the cause must in some way *necessitate* the effect. But no such necessary connection between the cause and the effect can possibly be observed, since, according to Hume, "there is no object, which implies the existence of any other if we consider these objects in themselves. . . ." Hence this necessitation must consist in a nomological, or lawlike, connection, viz., a uniformity in the behavior of "like objects."

> If objects had not an uniform and regular conjunction with each other, we shou'd never arrive at any idea of cause and effect. . . (I.3.i).

Since no event or existence is such that it logically implies or necessitates the existence of any other event, and since the causal relation has now been shown to be an external relation, and since all reasoning about external relations of events is "experimental," the same must be true of "causal inference."

Actions of the Mind

As we have seen, Hume's aim in the *Treatise* is to show that the experimental method of reasoning utilized in the natural sciences can be applied to *moral* subjects, and thus that a *moral science* is possible. Having shown, as he thought, that the experimental method of reasoning consists essentially of reasoning from objects present to the senses or memory, to the existence or relations of objects not so present, and that all such reasoning depends on the relation of causality or the *constant conjunction* of such objects, Hume's next step is to show that this same relation of constant conjunction is the foundation of our knowledge

of human actions, including both "the internal actions of
the mind" and publicly observable behavior or conduct.

Hume's argument takes it for granted that "our actions
have a constant union with our motives, tempers, and circumstances. . ." (II.3.i). Indeed, this circumstance is a condition of the possibility of social life and organization.

> There is a general course of nature in human actions,
> as well as in the operations of the sun and the climate.
> There are also characters peculiar to different nations and
> particular persons, as well as common to mankind. The
> knowledge of these characters is founded on the observa-
> tion of an uniformity in the actions, that flow from this. . .
> (*ibid.*).

Hume proceeds in this way because he thinks that no one
will dispute the claim that "actions have a constant union
and connexion with the situation and temper of the agent."
What he thinks will be disputed is the claim that this constant union or uniformity in human actions is sufficient for
asserting their *causality* in the same manner as events in
nature are caused. But Hume has already shown, as he believed, that the relation of cause and effect as it applies to
natural events consists of *nothing but* contiguity in space
or succession in time, and the relation of constant conjunction of similar objects. Thus the only way of eluding his
argument, that "in judging of the actions of men we must
proceed upon the same maxims, as when we reason concerning external objects," is by "denying that uniformity
of human actions, on which it is founded." Since he believes
that no one will wish to deny such an obvious fact, or be
committed to the apparent absurdities which would follow
from such a denial, he regards his argument as secure.

Hume's doctrine of the uniformity or causation of human
actions leads him to reject the traditional or theological
doctrine of the freedom of the human will. For Hume, an
action is free if and only if (1) it is caused by the agent's
conscious motives, or his desires and beliefs, and (2) there

is no external coercion or constraint on his behavior such that he is compelled to act in a way contrary to his own preferential desires. A man who is threatened by a robber and told to give up his money or his life might be said to have a choice, but his action, say, in giving up his money does not represent his preferential desire, which is to save *both* his money and his life. Hence his action would not be free in Hume's sense.

According to this theory, a necessary condition of a free action is that it be *caused* by the agent's desires and beliefs. This conflicts with the traditional doctrine of the freedom of the will because, according to that doctrine, a free agent cannot be caused to act as he does *by* any prior circumstances or state of affairs, including his internal or psychological states. In Hume's view, given a man's desires and beliefs and the particular circumstances of his action, what he does is the outcome or effect of those desires, beliefs, and circumstances. Hence, given those desires, beliefs, and circumstances, he *could not* have chosen or done otherwise.

Traditionalists object to Hume's account on the grounds that it is incompatible with our belief that men are *moral agents* and that they are *morally responsible* for their actions. From the traditional point of view, a man is not morally responsible for his action, and hence not a moral agent, unless *he could have chosen to do otherwise* even if his preferential desires were to do as he did. Thus if we accept Hume's account, we must also accept the consequence that human beings are not moral agents in the traditional or theological sense, and that they are not morally responsible for their actions. In a different sense of these terms, however, Hume could claim consistently with his doctrine of the causation of men's actions by their desires and beliefs, that they are morally free agents and morally responsible for their actions. A man can be said to be acting morally in Hume's sense if, among his desires, is the desire to do the morally correct thing, and this desire is preferential. And a man can be said to be morally responsible for his action if it is *possible* for him to desire to do the morally correct thing, and for this desire to be preferential. Thus a man who was brought to acknowledge that his past behavior in a particular case was morally reprehensible, might be motivated to avoid that kind of behavior in the future. In this way, it is always *possible* for a man to desire to act morally, even if at the time he acts he lacks any desire to do so.

The Relation of Reason to Action

According to Hume, there are two basic kinds of original perceptions or impressions: "impressions of sensation" and "reflective impressions." The first kind of impressions are "such as without any antecedent perception arise in the soul, from the constitution of the body, from the animal spirits, or from the application of objects to the external organs." Reflective impressions, on the other hand, "are such as proceed from some of these original ones, either immediately or by the interposition of its idea." These reflective impressions include all "bodily pains and pleasures" and "the passions, and other emotions resembling them" (II.1.i). Among the reflective impressions are "the sense of beauty and deformity in action, composition, and external objects," "the passions of love and hatred, grief and joy, pride and humility"; also "ambition, vanity, envy, pity, malice, generosity, with their dependants," as well as "desire, aversion, grief, joy, hope, fear, despair and security,"—in short, all the phenomena with which the moral sciences are concerned.

Now since our faculty of reason is nothing but the faculty of discovering truth or falsehood, and since the latter "consists in an agreement or disagreement either to the *real* relations of ideas, or to *real* existence and matter of fact," it follows that whatever is not "susceptible of this agreement or disagreement, is incapable of being true or false, and can never be an object of our reason." This apparently innocuous doctrine has important implications for the philosophy of social science. In the first place, it implies that neither the human actions studied by social science nor their causes are "beings of reason."

> ... 'tis evident our passions, volitions, and actions, are not susceptible of any such agreement or disagreement; being original facts and realities, compleat in themselves, and implying no reference to other passions, volitions, and actions. 'Tis impossible, therefore, they can be pronounced either true or false, and be either contrary or conformable to reason (III.1.i).

In other words, men's actions and passions are merely events like any other; they are not like *ideas* or *thoughts* which, in addition to being psychological events or dispositions, also have a *reference* to other events, such as impressions. We cannot, therefore, appraise actions and passions in the way we appraise ideas, i.e., as "agreeing or disagreeing with reality." It is only in virtue of their representational character that combinations of ideas can be said to be true or false, or that ideas can be said to stand for things that exist outside the imagination. But actions and passions are not copies of impressions; they are rather a kind of impression. Hence they are not representative of anything, but merely "original" existences. Since they can be neither true nor false, they are not "objects of reason"; since they are "original facts and realities," their existence cannot be appraised as "either contrary or conformable to reason." To say that a certain action is contrary or conformable to reason would be like saying that the existence of elephants and the non-existence of unicorns is either contrary or conformable to reason. But the existence of elephants and the non-existence of unicorns is neither a "more rational" nor a "less rational" state of affairs than the converse situation. Either situation is equally conceivable by the mind, and the question as to which obtains, cannot be answered merely by considering relations of ideas or what is discoverable *a priori*.

It seems to go against common use to say, as Hume does, that actions cannot be appraised as either "contrary or conformable to reason." After all, no way of speaking is more common than to refer to someone's behavior as "irrational." But Hume does not mean to contradict this way of speaking. His concern is merely to establish the proposition that actions are empirical facts, and that the existence of an action or a passion is a "brute fact" like any other empirical state of affairs. What he is denying is not that people's behavior may be appraised as rational or irrational, but that the causes of behavior, or the behavior itself, are *conclusions* of reason, which can be opposed to the "passions" in determining conduct.

Since human actions can be neither true nor false, and hence are not "beings of reason," the relation between a conclusion of reason and an action cannot be that of cause to effect. According to Hume, our faculty of reason is an instrument of the passions, i.e., of the reflective impressions. Consequently, although "reason and judgment may . . . be the mediate cause of an action, by prompting, or by directing a passion," only the latter can be the direct or immediate cause.

Thus Hume's teaching is that "reason is the slave of the passions," i.e., its function is purely instrumental in determining human behavior, the goal of behavior being always the satisfaction of particular desires or passions. Men's particular passions determine their particular goals, and reason influences behavior only in so far as men's ideas of the proper means to achieve their goals are arrived at by reasoning (II.2.iii).

In recent years, critics of Hume have pointed out what appears to be an absurd consequence of Hume's theory of action.[4] This consideration leads them to deny that human actions can be causally explained in any way. Their argument runs as follows. According to Hume, the connection between motives as causes and actions as effects is contingent. This is because every causal connection must be contingent. But to say that a causal connection is contingent implies that a given type of effect *conceivably* might not follow a given type of cause. Applying this to the relation between motives and actions, it follows, for instance, that *a man might intentionally benefit his enemy, although his beneficial action was motivated by revenge.* Since this appears to be a logical absurdity, these critics argue that while Hume's analysis of causality may be correct when applied to ordinary natural events, it is incorrect when applied to the analysis of the relation between motives and intentional human actions.

A similar objection is this. A man who *waves his hand* in order to make *a farewell gesture* is not doing two things but only one; to wave farewell is numerically the same event, in usual circumstances, as to wave one's hand. But Hume's theory requires us to call the hand-waving the *action* or *effect,* and the reason for doing it the *motive* or *cause;* hence if we accept Hume's theory we have to treat the hand-waving and the reason or motive for doing it as two separate events. This is because, in Hume's theory, the relation between cause and effect is a relation between distinct events. Since there are not two separate events in this kind of case, but only one event, Hume's theory must be incorrect as an account of the relation between motives and actions.

Furthermore, in Hume's theory the cause of an action is something internal or psychological, such as an act of will. But if an act of will is an event, then it too must have a cause, and this cause must be either an action or a non-action. If the precedent causal events are not all actions, as Hume's theory requires, then somewhere in the series there is an action which is the effect of a non-action. But *actions* must be distinguishable from events such as falling downstairs as a result of slipping on the landing. However, if both actions and non-actions are merely effects of events that befall us, we cannot make the required distinction. Thus Hume's theory requires us to treat intentional human actions as on a par with unintentional happenings that befall our bodies.

Where Hume's System Fails.

Hume, in the course of explaining his theory of our knowledge of the external world, remarks on the contrast between this sort of knowledge and the way in which we know our own minds.

> ... since all actions and sensations of the mind are known to us by consciousness, they must necessarily appear in every particular what they are, and be what they appear. Every thing that enters the mind, being in *reality* as the perception, 'tis impossible any thing shou'd to *feeling* appear different. This were to suppose, that even where we are most intimately conscious, we might be mistaken (I.4.ii).

In this passage, Hume seems to commit himself to the following propositions:

(1) *All* mental phenomena (actions and sensations of the mind) are known to us "by consciousness."

(2) We cannot be mistaken about what we know "by consciousness."

Hume is thinking here, of course, about the agent's knowledge of *his own mind and actions,* as opposed to his knowledge of the minds or actions of other persons. The kind of knowledge an agent has of his own mind or actions is often called introspective, and it is a feature of this kind of knowledge that it is not observational and experimental in Hume's sense. For example, if a man has a toothache, he does not have to make any observations or inferences in order to know that he has a toothache. He knows this just in virtue of undergoing the painful experience that we call toothache.

Hume fails to notice that this kind of non-observational, non-experimental knowledge cannot be extended to the minds or actions of other people, since *their* minds cannot be known to us by consciousness. He also fails to notice that the *infallibility* with which each person is supposed to know his own feelings and actions, is incompatible with his general thesis that our knowledge of human actions is of *the same kind* as our knowledge of the events of nature. For the latter kind of knowledge must be experimental and fallible. Clearly, the kind of knowledge an agent has of his own conscious experiences would be of no use for a moral or social *science,* which aims at a kind of knowledge which will be general, or true of every person or society, and which will be capable of verification by more than one person.[5] So the question arises, how does Hume propose to account for our knowledge of the minds and actions of other persons?

In a different part of the *Treatise,* Hume writes:

> We are conscious, that we ourselves, in adapting means to ends, are guided by reason and design, and that 'tis not ignorantly nor casually we perform those actions, which tend to self-preservation, to the obtaining pleasure, and avoiding pain. When therefore we see other creatures, in millions of instances, perform like actions, and direct them to like ends, all our principles of reason and probability carry us with an invincible force to believe in the existence of a like cause (I.3.xvi).

In other words, we can validly infer that other beings, whose behavior resembles our own, are conscious and have motives, sensations, etc., merely by observing their behavior and noting its similarity to our own. We can apply this same principle of reasoning, says Hume, to the question whether "beasts are endow'd with thought and reason as well as men." No truth appears to him more evident than that they are.

> 'Tis from the resemblance of the external actions of animals to those we ourselves perform, that we judge their internal likewise to resemble ours; and the same principle of reasoning, carry'd one step farther, will make us con-

clude that since our internal actions resemble each other, the causes, from which they are deriv'd, must also be resembling (*ibid.*) .

Unfortunately, any principle of reasoning which would enable us to infer validly that animals or other people have minds like our own would presuppose that we can have *ideas* of the "internal actions" of other beings. But we do not observe or otherwise experience any of the internal actions of other beings. What we can observe—and so have ideas of—are merely their bodily motions and their overt behavior. Since all ideas are derived from experience, and since we can never experience the internal actions of other minds, it appears to follow, on Hume's principles, that we can never even form the *idea* of an internal action of a mind which is not our own. If so, there is no basis even for any *probable* reasoning from premises about the similarity of other people's behavior to our own behavior, to the conclusion that the causes of their behavior must resemble our own conscious experiences.

According to Hume, if the cause of a perception is an idea, i.e., a perception caused in turn by an impression, then this perception should be classified as internal, or psychological, while if the cause is an "impression of the senses" and thus not itself caused by any idea, then it should be classified as an "external" perception. Since human actions are caused by men's motives, i.e., a species of internal perceptions, it follows that a science of human actions necessarily would be concerned with internal phenomena, such as motives. The physical sciences, on the other hand, being concerned solely with sense impressions or their objects, would be classified by Hume as dealing exclusively with external phenomena. So there is *this* difference, for Hume, between physical or natural sciences, and moral or social sciences: namely, that the latter are concerned with *both* internal and external phenomena, e.g., motives and behavior, and the former are concerned with external phenomena only. This, in fact, is Hume's *criterion* of a moral science, just as it was also J. S. Mill's.[6] But this way of distinguishing between the moral or social sciences, and the natural sciences, is fatal to the thesis of the unity of psychological and physical science.

If we assume that a plurality of minds or selves exist and that we can form ideas of the internal perceptions of other minds than our own, then we could justify inferences about the internal perceptions of others by analogy with our own behavior and the consciousness which attends it in similar circumstances. Although these are common sense assumptions, Hume is not entitled to make them, since he also assumes that all our ideas are derived from our own conscious experience.

The epistemological distinction between *internal* and *external* knowledge does not necessarily imply a metaphysical distinction between a world of mental events and a world of physical events. Indeed, it is doubtful that Hume is committed to the latter distinction, since for him all phenomena are basically of the same kind, which he called perceptions. The idea of a body as something specifically different from a perception, seemed to him an impossibility (I.2.vi). We either mean nothing at all by the word *body* or else we mean a set of associated perceptions, which we *imagine,* because of their "constancy" and "coherence," to exist unperceived (I.4.ii). Hume thought it was false, as a matter of fact, that any perceptions did exist unperceived; but he did not think that it was *logically* impossible that any should.[7] He saw no way of reconciling the inconsistency he found between the scientific theory of perception, according to which our perceptions are "caused" by "the action of bodies," which we do not perceive, and the common sense view that our perceptions are (sometimes) *identical* with physical objects. He therefore concluded that "there is a direct and total opposition betwixt our reason and our senses; or more properly speaking, betwixt those conclusions we form from cause and effect [namely, that our perceptions

are the effects of the action of bodies and our own physiological constitution], and those that persuade us of the
continu'd and independent existence of body" (I.4.iv). The
latter conclusions, he thought, were based merely on imagination.

Because of these and similar difficulties, many philosophers subsequent to Hume have sought to abolish, along
with the belief that there really is a mental world distinct
from a physical one, the distinction between internal and
external phenomena. This tendency is so prevalent that it is
often taken as a *sine qua non* of a "scientific attitude" in
the social sciences. What makes Hume so interesting in the
light of this contemporary attitude, is that he sought to
show that a science of human nature could be constructed
while preserving the common sense distinction between an
internal and an external world.[8] But he overlooked that by
his own showing, the direct deliverances of consciousness are
knowable only by the person whose consciousness it is. Yet
this is the *only* source he can find for our ideas of human
actions.

At the same time, according to Hume, neither consciousness, nor the "testimony of the sense and memory," can
possibly provide us with knowledge of the existence of anything not present to either, whether it is our own past and
future experiences, or the objects of the external world, or
the experiences of other beings. In the case of both the
internal and external worlds, the same kind of experimental
reasoning is needed in order to know of the existence of
objects beyond the immediate presentations of experience.

Hence, in Hume, our knowledge of moral phenomena in
so far as this includes the internal actions of other minds
than our own, both must be and yet cannot be experimental
and fallible. Thus Hume's doctrine of the unity of method
could not succeed. Even if we grant Hume that we might
justify our beliefs about the experiences of others by analogy
with our own behavior and experiences in similar circumstances, such beliefs could not be tested by observation and

experiment in the manner of the natural sciences. For the use of experiments in the moral sciences would have to be limited to introspective analysis and comparison, and the verification of a hypothesis could only be supplied by each individual in relation to the actions and sensations of his own mind.

III

Nineteenth and Early Twentieth Centuries

Hegel and Marx.

While it might be said that at the beginning of the nineteenth century philosophical thought about the social sciences had not advanced much beyond Hume, in the second quarter of that century two separate and conflicting schools of thought began to emerge, one led by John Stuart Mill in England, and the other led by G. W. F. Hegel (1770–1831) and afterwards by Karl Marx (1818–1883) in Germany.

Marx, proceeding on the basis of a critical study of Hegel and of the political economists such as Adam Smith, developed the view that the science of man and society should be conceived as theoretical history or the search for general laws of historical processes. Marx differed from Hegel, however, as to the nature of the primary causes of historical change or development. Hegel ascribed these changes to the work of "spirit" (*Geist*) as it manifested itself in human consciousness. For Hegel, social reality and social relations existed only in and through men's consciousness, which was therefore to be considered the field of history. Hegel thus distinguished sharply between history or social science, and nature or natural science, since the world of nature operated in accordance with mechanical laws and was independent of men's consciousness.

Marx, on the other hand, ascribed the primary causes of historical change to the material conditions of human existence, i.e., the actual forces of production, which, in his view, were responsible both for the forms of social organization and the forms of consciousness that characterized a given historical period. But Marx remained an Hegelian in his view that the forms of economic organization characterizing society at a particular time in history differed radically from such forms existing at other times. Thus for Marx, as well as for Hegel, human nature, in the eighteenth-century sense of this term, was a variable—subject to change in accordance with laws of historical development. It was the business of theoretical history (i.e., social science) to discover these laws and work out their consequences for given historical periods. These laws could be discovered, Marx thought, by investigating empirically the nature of the material conditions which prevailed at each historical period, and by then comparing the different periods. In Marx's view, as in Hegel's, history, or society, did not merely change; it *progressed* in accordance with directional or teleological laws, i.e., laws according to which change in history fulfilled a certain purpose or goal. For Hegel, this goal was the fulfillment of reason in history. For Marx, it was a rational and just social and economic organization which would enable individual human beings to fulfill their genuine needs and potentialities.

For Marx and Hegel, then, the kind of laws to be sought by a social science were laws of the historical process rather than psychological laws concerning the behavior or decisions of individual human agents. In other respects, however, Marx's thought diverged sharply from that of Hegel. While for Hegel the historical process consisted of the intended and unintended consequences of intentional human actions, and developed as a dialectical struggle of the "spirit," for Marx, history was a concrete, material process that developed only through conflict in the underlying forces of production that were not present to consciousness.

Marx is widely regarded today, both by his critics and apologists, as having repudiated philosophy. This opinion is supported by such comments as the following: "The question whether human thinking can reach objective truth is not a question of theory but a practical question. In practice man must prove the truth. . . . The dispute about the actuality or non-actuality of thinking—thinking isolated from practice—is a purely *scholastic* question." This Marxist thought is often believed to be a rejection of philosophy itself rather than merely a rejection of Hegelianism. This is because Marx's interpreters just assume that Marx is saying that *political activism is the only way of realizing truth.* But such a statement is self-refuting, since it is not itself an instance of political activism, and hence is false by its own criterion. Since Marx was not a philosophical novice, it is not reasonable to ascribe a plainly false view to him. What Marx should be understood as saying is that man reaches objective truth only insofar as he does *not* isolate thinking from practice or activity, i.e., correct philosophical thinking should be understood as an activity in its own right, which issues eventually in appropriate action. Similarly, when Marx says: "The philosophers have only *interpreted* the world in various ways; the point is, to *change* it,"—he should not be understood as saying that the task of interpreting the world is unimportant, nor even that this task is dispensable by those who wish to change the world. What Marx is saying is that the philosophical task of interpreting the world cannot be separated from the task of changing it, i.e., philosophical interpretation cannot be an end in itself without degenerating into scholasticism. It must be oriented towards improving the real conditions of human existence.[1]

J. S. Mill's Logic of Moral Inquiry.

John Stuart Mill, on the other hand, like Hume, tended to

think of social change on the analogy of physical change, and of historical progress or development as intentional human activity collectively considered, and carried on in accordance with invariant and universal psychological laws. For Mill and Hume, human nature is a constant; it does not vary from one historical period to another. It is not a product but a cause of historical change. In Mill's theory, for instance, each of the separate branches of social science— including history as the science of past social and political events—rested ultimately on "the science of mind" (or introspective psychology as we would call it today). Mill did, however, like Hegel and Marx, elaborate a theory of historical method which he thought was the only method of inquiry available to the "science of society." But unlike Marx and Hegel, Mill believed that the historical method could *not* be independent of nor the foundation of other sciences. For Mill, historical evidence ultimately had to be supported by facts and laws of psychological science, which were arrived at by the orthodox, experimental method of natural science. The real social variables, therefore, were neither "forms of consciousness" nor "economic substructures," but "states of society," each such state being determined by the particular circumstances of men and by the invariable structure of the human mind. Social and historical laws were derivative from more fundamental laws of individual psychology. For Mill, therefore, as for Hume, generalizations about social change and the development of social institutions were to be analyzed as generalizations about relations of individual human beings or their psychology.

Mill's *A System of Logic* appeared about a century after Hume's *Treatise*. It was an original attempt to provide a systematic and rigorous account of scientific method as such, abstracted from broader epistemological and metaphysical questions. Mill singled out the social sciences for special attention in the last or Sixth Book of the *Logic*, which he called "On the Logic of the Moral Sciences." The task of this work, as Mill described it, was merely to examine which of

> the methods of investigation of science in general are more especially suited to the various branches of moral inquiry; under what peculiar faculties or difficulties they are there employed; how far the unsatisfactory state of those inquiries is owing to a wrong choice of methods, how far to want of skill in the application of the right ones; and what degree of ultimate success can be attained or hoped for by a better choice and more careful employment of logical processes appropriate to the case. In other words, whether moral sciences exist, or can exist; to what degree of perfection they are capable of being carried; and by what selection or adaptation of the methods brought to view in the previous part of this work that degree of perfection is attainable (VI.1.ii).

Mill believed that he had exhaustively distinguished and explained the different kinds of method appropriate to scientific inquiry in the first five books of the *Logic*. Thus he was able to write, in the sixth book: ". . . the methods of investigation applicable to moral and social science must have been already described, if I have succeeded in enumerating those of science in general" (*ibid.*). In asserting this conclusion, Mill in effect denied that the social sciences gave rise to any substantial problems that were not also encountered in a philosophical consideration of the methods of the natural sciences. Mill does not make an extensive attempt to defend this thesis, however, and so far as he does offer a defense of it, his arguments do not really go beyond those already given by Hume a hundred years previously. Mill went beyond Hume in making an explicit division of the *moral sciences* into psychology, on the one hand, and social science, properly speaking, on the other. He regarded psychology as the science of individual human actions, thoughts, and feelings, and the social sciences, properly speaking, as sciences of the "collective actions of mankind." Mill also went beyond Hume in attempting to specify certain methods of scientific inquiry which would be especially appropriate to social as opposed to natural sciences.

Durkheim's Scientific Sociology

Émile Durkheim (1858–1917), who is often referred to as the founder of scientific sociology, once wrote, in a passage that is now quite well known and often quoted: [2]

> I consider extremely fruitful this idea that social life should be explained, not by the notions of those who participate in it, but by more profound causes which are unperceived by consciousness, and I think also that these causes are to be sought mainly in the manner according to which the associated individuals are grouped. Only in this way, it seems, can history become a science, and sociology itself exist.

Durkheim's reference, of course, is to Marx's materialist conception of history. T. B. Bottomore has pointed out: [3]

> ... according to Durkheim the validity of this conception was in no way connected with the destiny of a political movement, since in any case he himself had arrived at this view before reading Marx, and the whole development of historiography and psychology in the last half-century [i.e., the last half of the nineteenth century] had been towards this "objective" conception of history, which should not be identified with historical materialism.

While Durkheim's view should not be *identified* with Marx's theory of history, the "idea that social life should be explained, not by the notions of those who participate in it," but by "causes which are unperceived by consciousness," was first elaborated in any detail by Marx and Engels in their *Deutsche Ideologie*. There is no need to be sceptical of Durkheim's claim to have arrived at this view independently, however. A more important consideration, for our purposes, is Durkheim's remark that adopting such a view seems to be *necessary* if "sociology," i.e., social science, is to be possible. As we saw in examining Hume, the assumption that social life could be explained by appealing to psychological facts about human individuals encountered the difficulty that the kind of knowledge we have of our own experiences seems to be quite different from the kind of knowledge we have of the events of nature or the external world. Hume's attempt to show that the experimental method of reasoning of the natural sciences could be applied to the study of social life failed for this reason. Durkheim is here explicitly asserting that the condition of the possibility of a social science is explaining social life by causes "which are unperceived by consciousness," i.e., by non-psychological factors. According to Durkheim, these causes are to be found "in the manner according to which the associated individuals are grouped." Durkheim suggests that a study of this kind of grouping would reveal a set of *societal* facts which would be independent of psychology, and which could provide the foundation of an autonomous science of society. Thus the epistemological problems of our knowledge of our own minds and the minds of others would be by-passed.

In order to come to grips with Durkheim's thesis, let us list some of the important concepts and propositions which occur in his statement.

(1) The concept of *social life*.

(2) The concept of *the manner according to which the associated individuals are grouped*.

(3) The concept of *explaining social life* (by one method or another).

(4) The concept of human beings who *participate* in social life, and who have *notions* (ideas) about what social life is and why they participate in it as they do.

(5) The proposition that the *causes of social life* are *unperceived by consciousness,* i.e., they do not belong among the "notions" of participants. (Hence these causes would not be psychological—would not be found in an inventory of the consciousness or mind of any individual.)

(6) The proposition that it is a necessary condition of the existence of a social science that social life should *not* be explained by the ideas of participants, but by reference to other factors.

(7) The proposition that the causes of social life, in terms of which sociological explanations should be given, probably are to be found in some set of uniquely societal facts (i.e., "the manner according to which the associated individuals are grouped").

It follows from (5), (6), and (7) that "participants" are not usually conscious of "the manner according to which they are grouped." Presumably, this would be something that the sociologist would be able to discover about them, by empirical investigation.

Durkheim tacitly assumes, furthermore, that:

(8) The people who participate in social life do have ideas about the latter; and

(9) *They* would explain their social life by these ideas.

It follows, then, that the explanations of participants would only be a datum for the social scientist, since the latter, according to Durkheim, in giving *his* explanations, must disregard the ideas of participants.

Furthermore, it follows from proposition (6) above that:

(10) If, in the nature of the case, we are limited to explaining social life by the notions of those who participate in it, then (according to Durkheim), history cannot become a science, nor can scientific sociology exist.

If, on the other hand, (10) should be false, then so must (6), since (6) purports to state a necessary condition of the existence of scientific sociology.

Now Durkheim may have been wrong in espousing the view represented in (10), although it is one that is very widely accepted by social scientists. So the weight of authority is on the side of Durkheim. But, for the moment, it is not the truth or falsity of this view which interests us, but the reasons for believing it. Let us take (10) as the focus of our discussion, since it is principally on the basis of (10) that Durkheim's view takes on special interest and importance.

Ordinarily, when we think of the nature of social science, we do not suppose that in order to give acceptable explanations of social life, the ideas of participants *must* be disregarded. Indeed, there are some social scientists who would claim precisely the opposite. But if (10) is true, then the latter group of social scientists, if they are using the term *science* in the same manner as Durkheim, must agree that history or sociology can never become a science. (By *history* in this context is meant descriptions of actual human conduct, or of changes which have occurred in men's social and political institutions as a result of such conduct.)

Suppose, however, that Durkheim is wrong in asserting (10), i.e., suppose that the following are both true:

(A) Social life cannot be explained *except* by the notions of those who participate in it;

(B) If we do explain social life by the notions of those who participate in it, then history and sociology *can* exist.

In other words, imagine an anti-Durkheim, who had had a similar influence over the research faculties of universities, and who had written as follows:

> I consider extremely fruitful this idea that social life should be explained primarily by the notions of those who participate in it, and that causes which are unperceived by consciousness should be used to explain social life only when the ideas of participants are not available, and I think also that these ideas are to be sought mainly in the conventions and rules to which the associated individuals consciously or habitually adhere in their conduct. Only in this way, it seems, can there be a historical science, or sociology itself exist.

This view of an imaginary anti-Durkheim is not so remote from reality as may appear; on the contrary, as we shall see, Weber and other interpretationists would tend to characterize social studies in just such terms. We shall discuss Weber's views at some length in the next section.

Our consideration of the possibility of an anti-Durkheim makes evident one important point: We can conceive of a social science which permits or enjoins explanations of social life in terms of the ideas and beliefs of participants. The *idea* of a social science which sought to provide explanations in terms of participant ideas is not inconsistent or absurd. Durkheim's rejection of this idea of a social science is a consequence of the assumptions he makes regarding the conditions of the possibility of a social science. First, he assumes that the experimental method of reasoning, in Hume's sense, is logically inappropriate for establishing results about ideas of participants. Secondly, he assumes that this method of reasoning is essential to any science which restricts itself to the investigation of matters of fact that cannot be known *a priori* or by consciousness alone. Finally, he assumes that when we use the term *science,* unqualified in any way, what we mean is a science which utilizes the experimental method of reasoning, i.e., a natural science.

This point is important because of the verbal confusion which may result when it is alleged that a social science is (or is not) possible. If we agree with Durkheim, both this sentence and its negation would have entirely different logical consequences from what they would have if we agree with our anti-Durkheim. From the former point of view, to say that a social science is possible, is to say that we can fruitfully apply experimental methods in social studies, and that we must ignore or disregard the thoughts and beliefs of participants. From the latter point of view, it is to say that although the experimental method cannot be fruitfully applied in social studies, since we *must* take account of ideas of participants—a method is available that *can* be employed fruitfully in social inquiries, viz., the method of *verstehen* or interpretive understanding. (This method will be discussed in the next section.)

Thus the disputed point between the Durkheim and anti-

Durkheim schools of thought is not whether a science of society is possible, for it *is* possible on both views. Rather, what is being disputed is whether a social science must use the ideas of participants in framing its explanations. The belief that if we must use their ideas, then we cannot employ an experimental method in social inquiries (except incidentally) is common both to the Durkheim and the anti-Durkheim schools of thought.

If we now consider the unity of method thesis discussed in the first chapter, we can see how this thesis fails to come to grips with what Durkheim identifies as the central methodological problem of the social sciences. A similar criticism applies to Mill. Indeed, Mill's defense of the unity of method amounts to little more than just *assuming* that scientific method as utilized in the natural sciences can be applied to the study of society, and deducing the implications of this assumption. Since Mill conceives of society as nothing but the resultant of psychological causes, he just assumes what Durkheim explicitly denies. Hume, on the other hand, as we saw in chapter II, at least tried to show that "events of consciousness" could be investigated by the experimental method.

Max Weber and Interpretive Sociology.

After Durkheim, the next major influence on the philosophy of the social sciences stemmed from the work of Max Weber (1864–1920). Weber's approach to the problems of social science is quite different from that of Hume and Mill, and in some ways is more akin to that of Hegel. Hume and Mill held that all knowledge is derived from observational experience, and that this experience consists in sensations or perceptions. Weber, on the other hand, is influenced by the tradition of German Idealism which emphasized the independence of conceptual thinking from sensation. Although Weber never wrote a systematic treatise on the methodology of the social sciences, his views are available in several essays, written at different periods of his life. His best known work is *The Protestant Ethic and the Spirit of Capitalism,* which is as much a philosophical as a scientific treatise.[4]

According to Weber, when we are concerned with a social science, what we have in mind is a science of "social action," which consists in "meaningful behavior." [5] The latter cannot be studied merely by observation as in physical sciences, but must include a method of "interpretive understanding" or *verstehen.* Explanation in social science aims not merely at laying bare the causes but also at making historical and social events humanly understandable, in terms of their motives, value-attributions, and significance as these are understood by the human agents involved.

Weber makes a strong distinction between "factual" and "valuational" judgments, and argues that the social sciences must avoid offering value-judgments as if they were statements of scientific fact. This distinction, which has been the focus of endless controversy, is not original with Weber and may be traced back to Mill and Hume. According to Weber, the propositions of social science are not value-judgments; they are factual or descriptive propositions which require that they be "verified" just as do the hypotheses of the physical sciences. Nevertheless, the social sciences are "value-dependent" in a way that the natural sciences are not. This is because the *cultural* significance of events, which the social scientist is mainly interested in studying, has no "objective" existence in nature, i.e., it is not an observable or physical property. Furthermore, according to Weber, generalization and explanation in social science must make use of certain unique conceptual constructions, which he calls "ideal types." These ideal types are not statements of fact, but they have somewhat the same function in social science that physical laws have in natural science, i.e., they supply the premises of sociological explanations.[6]

Weber believed that the social sciences are distinguished from the natural sciences mainly by the fact that the former study social events from the standpoint of how these events were influenced by the ideas or beliefs of participants. Weber seems to have been led to this view as a result of his researches into the historical connection between the rise of modern industrial capitalism and Protestant ethical and religious beliefs.

Weber defined sociology as a "science which attempts the interpretive understanding of social action in order thereby to arrive at a causal explanation of its course and effects." Weber also says that interpretive understanding is "the specific characteristic of sociological knowledge." Weber's formulations imply that the aim of social science is the causal explanation of the course and effects of social actions, and that interpretive understanding of such action is *necessary* in order to fulfill this aim.

Weber was led to propose this definition of sociology as a result of reflecting on the question: what specific kinds of events would be of interest to a sociological investigator? Clearly, not every type of contact of human beings has a *social* character. Weber considers the example of two people riding their bicycles who collide. The mere collision of the cyclists, he says, may be compared to a natural event, i.e., it would not be the sort of event that would interest the social scientist. "On the other hand," he goes on to say, "their attempt to avoid hitting each other, or whatever insults, blows, or friendly discussion might follow the collision," would constitute events of the type that sociologists study; that is, these latter events would be cases or instances of social action.

Weber distinguishes between *individual action* and *social action*. He defines the terms *action* and *social action* as follows:

> In 'action' is included all human behavior when and in so far as the acting individual attaches a subjective meaning to it. Action in this sense may be either overt or purely inward or subjective; it may consist of positive intervention in a situation, or of deliberately refraining from

such intervention or passively acquiescing in the situation.

Action is social in so far as, by virtue of the subjective meaning attached to it by the acting individual (or individuals), it takes account of the behavior of others, and is thereby oriented in its course.

What Weber understands by the term *subjective meaning* may be gathered from the example of the cyclists. Suppose one cyclist swerves suddenly from his path, just as he becomes aware that another cyclist is approaching him on a collision course. Then part of the *subjective meaning* of the swerve would be that the first cyclist *intended* to avoid hitting the second. The swerve would have this subjective meaning even if it should turn out that the cyclists collide. On the other hand, the same kind of swerve, considered merely as a natural event, might have occurred in a similar situation when it did not have this subjective meaning. For example, the first cyclist could be intoxicated and just happen to swerve as the second cyclist was approaching, but without the intention of avoiding the latter. Further examples could be provided. Weber's point is that in the case of a social action, understanding the subjective or intended meaning of the observable behavior is essential to giving an adequate explanation of why it occurred.

According to Weber, social action "may be oriented to the past, present, or expected future behavior of others." The others in question may be "individual persons" or they may constitute "an indefinite plurality and may be entirely unknown as individuals." Thus money is a "means of exchange which the actor accepts in payment because he orients his action to the expectation that a large but unknown number of individuals . . . will be ready to accept it in exchange on some future occasion." Economic transactions are therefore meaningful in Weber's sense. But not all behavior is meaningful. For example, a man who senses that he is falling will instinctively react by stiffening his limbs. This would be a case of what Weber calls "merely reactive behavior," i.e., behavior whose explanation does not require a reference to the agent's own understanding of what he is doing. Although "the line between meaningful action and merely reactive behavior to which no subjective meaning is attached, cannot be sharply drawn empirically," the distinction is nevertheless important. Merely reactive behavior, or the sort of behavior which is a result of either innate or conditioned reflexes, is usually not investigated by sociologists. At the time Weber was writing, i.e., during the first quarter of the twentieth century, psychology was beginning to occupy itself almost exclusively with *merely reactive* as opposed to *meaningful* behavior. Weber's aim, in part, was probably to make conceptually clear the distinction we commonly presuppose between psychology as the science of behavior and sociology as the science of society. If we look back on Hume's concerns from the perspective of Weber's time, we can see that, although Hume made no attempt to distinguish formally between these two kinds of behavior, he was often concerned specifically with what Weber calls meaningful action as opposed to merely reactive behavior. In so far as Hume attempted to construct a *moral science* or was concerned specifically with *moral phenomena,* his interests could be described as *sociological* in Weber's sense.

In Weber's view, specifically meaningful behavior, or action, is always "subjectively understandable." To use our example of the cyclists—we gather from observing the circumstances of this event that the swerving motion of the first cyclist was aimed at avoiding a collision, because we would have done the same kind of thing in similar circumstances, and for similar reasons. In other words, we *understand* the swerving of the cyclist as an *action* with this or that *meaning,* by extending to this event the direct understanding we would have of our own behavior in similar circumstances. Thus Weber uses the term *understanding* to refer to the kind of knowledge we have of our own experiences, intentions, thoughts, emotions, sensations, and so on. Strictly speaking, only each person's *understanding* of his own behavior is *subjective*. When we extend this kind of understanding to the behavior of others, Weber calls it *interpretive understanding*. Although understanding in this sense is a kind of mental act which occurs in "the context of discovery," as empiricists say, it does not follow that such mental acts are irrelevant to the "context of justification." Just as sensory observation in natural science plays a role *both* in the context of justification and the context of discovery, so interpretive understanding, for Weber, is involved in both contexts in the social sciences.

Weber distinguishes two kinds of interpretive understanding. First, there is "the direct observational understanding *(aktuelles Verstehen)* of the subjective meaning of a given act as such, including verbal utterances." Thus we understand in this sense "the meaning of the proposition $2 \times 2 = 4$ when we hear or read it." We also understand in this sense "an outbreak of anger as manifested by facial expression, exclamations or irrational movements. . . . We can understand in a similar observational way the action of a woodcutter or of somebody who reaches for the knob to shut a door or who aims a gun at an animal." When Weber speaks here of *direct observational understanding* he does not mean, of course, mere sensory observation. What he means is that in cases such as understanding an outbreak of anger as manifested by someone's facial expression, we are not conscious of making any *inferences* from the facial expression to the angry feeling. We report actions of this kind just as if we could directly observe them. Thus when we observe someone applying an ax to a log in successive rapid motions, we are not conscious of inferring that he has the intention of chopping the wood; we feel that we are able to understand his intention directly or without inference.

The second kind of interpretive understanding is called "explanatory understanding" *(erklärendes Verstehen)*. This is the kind of understanding we have of an action when

... we understand in terms of *motive* the meaning an actor attaches to the proposition twice two equals four, when he states it or writes it down.... we understand what makes him do this at precisely this moment and in these circumstances. Understanding in this sense is attained if we know that he is engaged in balancing a ledger or in making a scientific demonstration, or is engaged in some other task of which this particular act would be an appropriate part. This ... understanding ... consists in placing the act in an intelligible and more inclusive context of meaning.

Thus whereas we have direct observational understanding of the meaning of the proposition $2 \times 2 = 4$ when we read or hear it, or of the action of a man chopping wood, we do not necessarily understand, say, *why* this particular proposition is being spoken or written, or *why* the man is chopping wood. But when we place the action in "a more inclusive context of meaning" we can understand these matters also.

Thus we understand the chopping of wood or aiming of a gun in terms of motive in addition to direct observation if we know that the wood chopper is working for a wage or is chopping a supply of firewood for his own use or possibly is doing it for recreation. But he might also be 'working off' a fit of rage.... Similarly we understand the motive of a person aiming a gun if we know that he has been commanded to shoot as a member of a firing squad, that he is fighting against an enemy, or that he is doing it for revenge.... Finally we have a motivational understanding of the outburst of anger if we know that it has been provoked by jealousy, injured pride, or an insult.... In all the above cases the particular act has been placed in an understandable sequence of motivation, the understanding of which can be treated as an explanation of the actual course of behavior. Thus for a science which is concerned with the subjective meaning of action, explanation requires a grasp of the complex of meaning in which an actual course of understandable action thus interpreted belongs.

Explanatory understanding, Weber goes on to say,

... involves the interpretive grasp of the meaning present in one of the following contexts: (a) as in the historical approach, the actually intended meaning for concrete individual action; or (b) as in the case of sociological mass phenomena the average of, or an approximation to, the actually intended meaning; or (c) the meaning appropriate to a scientifically formulated pure type (an ideal type) of a common phenomenon.

For example, in the case of the historical explanation of the action of a particular person, say Caesar's crossing of the Rubicon, the *meaning* of the action consists of Caesar's intentions, motives, thoughts, etc., or the propositional content of these items; and the implications of this action for the political situation of the Roman Empire at that time. When we are concerned with a "sociological mass phenomenon," on the other hand, such as the rise of industrial capitalism in Western Europe between the sixteenth and twentieth centuries, the *meaning* of this phenomenon consists in an "average of, or an approximation to, the actually intended meaning" of the actions of each of the many individuals involved. The third kind of case that Weber has in mind is illustrated by the concepts and laws of pure economic theory. The laws of economics, according to Weber, state "what course a given type of action would take if it were strictly rational, unaffected by errors or emotional factors and if, furthermore, it were completely and unequivocally directed to a single end, the maximization of economic advantage." These laws, then, express "the meaning appropriate to a scientifically formulated pure type [i.e., an "ideal type," to use Weber's technical term] of a common phenomenon." Weber uses the term *ideal type* in this kind of context in order to convey the fact that the theoretical formulations of the economist are not literally *descriptive* of the course of events. This is because, for example, most cases of actual economic behavior do not in fact maximize economic advantage, either because people are not ideally rational or because they often have other motivations than merely economic ones.

While in all these cases explanatory interpretation "attempts to attain clarity and certainty," the mere fact that we have arrived at a plausible interpretation is not enough to insure that it is a "causally valid interpretation," i.e., that the explanation provided by the understanding is true. So long as we remain only on "the level of meaning," Weber says, we have only a "peculiarly plausible hypothesis." For instance, in the case of the historical explanation of a particular action, an agent's "conscious motives may well, even to the actor himself, conceal the various motives and repressions which constitute the real driving force of his action." In that case "even subjectively honest self-analysis has only a relative value." In other words, an agent's understanding of his own motives may well be erroneous or inadequate. "Then it is the task of the sociologist to be aware of this motivational situation," Weber says, "and to describe and analyse it, even though it has not actually been concretely part of the conscious 'intention' of the actor. . . ."

For these and similar reasons, "verification of subjective interpretation by comparison with the concrete course of events" is necessary. But how can we verify or test empirically a particular subjective interpretation? In some cases, Weber says, we can apply psychological experimentation, but this kind of procedure is obviously not available for testing hypotheses about past social and historical events. For sociological mass phenomena, verification can be provided only by the available statistical evidence. In addition to psychological experimentation and statistical confirmation, there remains only the relatively inconclusive procedure "of comparing the largest possible number of historical or contemporary processes which, while otherwise similar, differ in one decisive point of their relation to the particular motive or factor the role of which is being investigated."

By the term *verification* in this context, Weber merely means a procedure of *checking* or *backing up* the claim that an interpretive hypothesis correctly represents the actual course of history, or the causes of the social processes under study. For example, Weber's own interpretive hypothesis that Protestant ethical and religious beliefs helped to determine the development of the economic institutions of capitalistic societies in Western Europe, can be backed up by statistical evidence which shows that the percentage of Protestants in the upper ranks of skilled labor and positions of management in large industrial corporations is greater by far than their proportion in the total population of the affected nations.

Although verification by available statistical evidence is necessary, according to Weber, the evidence, in the absence of interpretation, will leave "our need for causal understanding . . . unsatisfied." In other words, understanding the meaning of an action or social process is necessary, according to Weber, in order to explain it causally. The premises of the causal explanation must refer to the motives of the agents and the social context in which their actions are placed. On the other hand, any acceptable interpretation must also be shown to be "in some degree relevant to an actual course of action." Otherwise, an interpretive hypothesis would fail to be explanatory, i.e., it would be "worthless for the understanding of action in the real world." In some cases, however, "the correspondence between the theoretical interpretation of motivation and its empirical verification is entirely satisfactory," and "the cases are numerous enough so that verification can be considered established."

Weber distinguishes between the "causal adequacy" of an explanatory hypothesis and its "adequacy on the level of meaning." An hypothesis is causally adequate if it states the sufficient conditions of the occurrence of the action. But genuine explanatory understanding, including causally adequate understanding, requires reference to the agents' motives for the action. For Weber, a "motive is a complex of subjective meaning which seems to the actor himself or to the observer an adequate ground for the conduct in question." Thus a reference to a motive is necessarily a reference to participant ideas in Durkheim's sense. Hence a motive-explanation which did not refer to participant ideas would be logically impossible, from Weber's point of view.

In order to understand a course of social action, we must understand how the agents involved in it understood what they were doing. Thus explanatory understanding in social science requires, in addition to causal adequacy, "adequacy on the level of meaning." An interpretation of a course of conduct is adequate on the level of meaning, Weber says, "when and in so far as, according to our habitual modes of thought and feeling, its component parts taken in their mutual relation . . . constitute a 'typical' complex of meaning." For example, the swerving of the cyclist is interpreted by the observer as an attempt to avoid collision, the latter being an instance of a "typical complex of meaning" in accordance with our "habitual modes of thought and feeling." Such an interpretation will not be *causally adequate,* however, unless, "according to established generalizations from experience, there is a probability that it will always actually occur in the same way." In other words, causal understanding implies an element of universality, or causal laws. This view of causal understanding is close to Hume's. Thus our interpretation of the cyclist's swerve is causally adequate only if there is a significantly greater probability that anyone in the same circumstances would act in the same way as our cyclist, than that he would act in a different way.

The aim of social inquiry, then, is "correct causal interpretation of a concrete course of action." This is arrived at "when the overt action and the motives have both been correctly apprehended and at the same time their relation has become meaningfully comprehensible." Thus the relation between the motive of the cyclist, to avoid collision, and the consequent intentional swerving of his bicycle—the overt action—is meaningfully comprehensible. Other possible interpretations should be compared and considered in the light of all the evidence, before we advance one in particular as explanatory. But if "adequacy in respect to meaning is lacking, then no matter how . . . precisely its probability can be numerically determined," the hypothesis is still not explanatory; it is merely a "statistical probability." For example, the numerical probability of the number of serious injuries resulting from bicycle collisions in the United States for next year, could probably be fairly precisely determined. But this would not give us an explanatory understanding of these accidents. Statistical uniformities constitute "understandable types of action" and thus provide "sociological generalizations," according to Weber, "only when they can be regarded as manifestations of the understandable subjective meaning of a course of social action." This is precisely what would be lacking in the case of the bicycle collision statistics, as well as in the case of real statistical uniformities such as the drowning rate or the suicide rate in various countries. On the other hand, statistics showing a disproportionately large number of Protestants in the upper ranks of skilled labor and positions of management in large industrial corporations, was shown by Weber to be a manifestation of "an understandable subjective meaning of a course of social action" in his studies on *The Protestant Ethic and the Spirit of Capitalism*.

> There are statistics of processes devoid of meaning such as death rates, phenomena of fatigue, the production rates of machines, the amount of rainfall, in exactly the same sense as there are statistics of meaningful phenomena. But only when the phenomena are meaningful is it convenient to speak of sociological statistics. Examples are such cases as crime rates, occupational distributions, price statistics, and statistics of crop acreage. Naturally there are many cases where both components are involved, as in crop statistics.

Although social action, "in the sense of subjectively understandable orientation of behavior exists only as the behavior of one or more *individual* human beings," social action is often attributed to institutions or what Weber calls "social collectivities," such as states, associations, business corporations, foundations, etc. While it may be "convenient or even indispensable to treat social collectivities . . . as if they were individual persons," or as if they were "subjects of rights and duties or . . . performers of legally significant actions," these collectivities must be regarded as *"solely* the resultants and modes of organization of the particular acts of individual persons. . . ." This is because "subjectively understandable" behavior or action can only be actions of individuals. We cannot literally attribute motives, intentions, etc., to institutions considered as totalities or wholes without encountering absurdities.

The concepts of collective entities such as the state, the nation, corporations, the family, etc., "have a meaning in the minds of individual persons," Weber says, "partly as of something actually existing, partly as something with normative authority."

> This is true not only of judges and officials, but of ordinary private individuals as well. Actors thus in part orient their action to them, and in this role such ideas have a powerful, often a decisive, causal influence on the course of action of real individuals. This is above all true where the ideas concern a recognized positive or negative normative pattern. Thus, for instance, one of the important aspects of the 'existence' of a modern state, precisely as a complex of social interaction of individual persons, consists in the fact that the action of various individuals is oriented to the belief that it exists or should exist, thus that its acts and laws are valid in the legal sense.

If so, characteristics investigated by the sociologist such as the *legitimacy* of the modern state, or conversely, its loss of *legitimacy* in the eyes of the people, are matters that can be treated only from the standpoint of interpretive understanding. For this property only exists so far as people *believe* that it does; it is their collective belief in its legitimacy or illegitimacy that *confers* those characteristics, in their empirical existence.

According to Weber, when we are dealing with social collectivities or institutions, the sociologist is in a position "to go beyond merely demonstrating functional relationships and uniformities," i.e., beyond merely giving deductive causal-theoretic explanations. The sociologist can accomplish something "which is never attainable in the natural sciences, namely the subjective understanding of the actions of the component individuals."

> The natural sciences ... cannot do this, being limited to the formulation of causal uniformities in objects and events and the explanation of individual facts by applying them. We do not 'understand' the behavior of cells, but can only observe the relevant functional relationships and generalize on the basis of these observations. This additional achievement of explanation by interpretive understanding, as distinguished from external observation, is of course attained only at a price—the more hypothetical and fragmentary its results. Nevertheless, subjective understanding is the specific characteristic of sociological knowledge.

Weber explicitly denies that by *"verstehen"* he is referring to a *faculty* which is separate and distinct from our usual faculties of sensory observation and understanding. Accordingly, many commentators have interpreted him as referring to a psychological process of empathy which, although it may have a valuable heuristic function, cannot be any part of the logical process of justifying hypotheses.[7] This interpretation has distorted Weber's doctrine. *"Verstehen"* may involve empathy, but the latter is neither necessary nor sufficient; it is observation of a different *kind* from that which is involved in contexts where what is being observed are events devoid of cultural significance. To see this, consider an analogous case. Gilbert Ryle speaks of different kinds of *attending,* e.g., humming a tune with concentration and humming a tune absentmindedly.[8] Humming a tune with concentration, he says, is not doing *two* things: humming and concentrating, but only one. In the same way, interpreting a social event is not doing two things, observing and understanding, but only one: observing it *with* understanding.

Now anything whatever can be observed with understanding; but there are some things that must be understood just in order to be observed. And there are two ways in which this may be so. In one way, what we mean is that the *observer* must have the appropriate understanding, but we do not imply that *what* is being understood is itself something that has understanding or has a meaning to someone. This is the case in the natural sciences. In the social sciences, however, understanding what a person or a group *understands* may be necessary in order to observe or explain their social practices. We sometimes use the word *understands* in this way to apply to groups, e.g., "What do the Trobriand Islanders understand by *kinship?*" And the answer, if complete and detailed, constitutes a description and an explanation of their social institution of kinship relations. Now the activity of observing, in contexts where what is understood has a *meaning* to the agents being observed, is typically the sort of activity to which Weber applied the concept of *"verstehen"*, i.e., the activity of taking into account for explanatory purposes either what *meaning* the agent or agents attach to their actions, or what *meaning* is attached to their actions by the social or institutional framework in which they live. Thus the concept of *"verstehen"* may be regarded as a variety of *heeding* or attending to something, whose character derives essentially from the fact that it belongs to an institutional setting or a context of conventions.

Criticisms of Weber.

As we mentioned in chapter I, empiricism holds that all scientific knowledge must be completely expressible in the hypothetical-deductive form of natural science. So an empiricist would not accept Weber's account of interpretive understanding as implying the falsehood or unacceptability of the unity of method thesis. Thus Carl G. Hempel, a contemporary logical empiricist, has written as follows: [9]

> In natural science, to explain a unique concrete event ... amounts to showing that it had to be expected in view of certain other concrete events which are prior to or contemporaneous with it, and by virtue of specifiable general laws or theories. Formally, such explanation consists in the deduction of [a statement describing the unique concrete event] from those general principles and from the 'boundary conditions' describing the antecedent and contemporaneous occurrences.

Hempel proceeds to comment explicitly on Weber's thesis that sociological knowledge and explanation differ from the kind that is provided in the natural sciences.

> As Max Weber's writings clearly show, an adequate explanation of a concrete event in sociology or historiography has to be of essentially the same character. Reliance on empathic insight and subjective 'understanding' provides no warrant of objective validity, no basis for the systematic prediction or postdiction of specific phenomena; the latter procedures have to be based on general empirical rules, on nomological knowledge. Weber's limitation of the explanatory principles of sociology to 'meaningful' rules of intelligible behavior, on the other hand, is untenable: many, if not all, occurrences of interest to the social scientist require, for their explanation, reference to factors which are 'devoid of subjective meaning', and accordingly also to 'non-understandable uniformities', to use Weber's terminology. Weber acknowledges that the sociologist must accept such facts as causally significant data, but he insists that this does 'not in the least alter the specific task of sociological analysis . . . , which is the interpretation of action in terms of its subjective meaning.' But this conception bars from the field of sociology any theory of behavior which foregoes the use of 'subjectively meaningful' motivational concepts. This either means a capricious limitation of the concept of sociology—which, as a result, might eventually become inapplicable to any phase of scientific

research—or else it amounts to an *a priori* judgment on the character of any set of concepts which can possibly yield explanatory sociological theories. Clearly, such an *a priori* verdict is indefensible, and indeed, the more recent development of psychological and social theory shows that it is possible to formulate explanatory principles for purposive action in purely behavioristic, non-introspective terms.

Hempel's criticism of Weber's thesis is based partly on a misunderstanding of that thesis and partly on an alternative approach to social science whose possibility is never denied by Weber.

In the first place, Weber does not claim that it is impossible either to assign physical meanings to social terms, or to dispense with social terms altogether. Rather, he provides an analysis of a kind of knowledge we already possess and that obviously belongs to the social sciences. Presumably, we should, in our *theory* of science, attempt to describe and explain epistemological features of branches of knowledge that already exist. The present situation in the social sciences demands that we often mention people's ideas as well as use them in giving explanations of social events. It is this *logical* characteristic of social hypotheses that Weber is trying to explicate. Thus Weber writes:

It is altogether possible that future research may be able to discover non-understandable uniformities [i.e. causal-theoretic uniformities] underlying what has appeared to be specifically meaningful action. . . .

This passage *precedes* the one quoted by Hempel and puts the latter in a more tenable context. Thus Weber goes on to say,

The recognition of the causal significance of such factors would naturally not in the least alter the specific task of sociological analysis or that of the other sciences of action, which is the interpretation of action in terms of its subjective meaning. The effect would be only to introduce certain non-understandable data of the same order as others which, it has been noted . . . , are already present, into the complex of subjectively understandable motivation at certain points.

Hempel's claim that in the future we will be able to formulate explanatory principles for purposive action in purely behavioristic, non-introspective terms, depends for its appeal partly on the belief that the kind of knowledge Weber tries to describe is "imperfect," as judged by standards of natural science. But Weber argues that the aim of sociology is to give true or factually satisfactory explanations of events whose differentiation at least sometimes involves the recognition that a "subjective sense" is attached to them. From his standpoint, what constitutes a science is the ability to produce satisfactory explanations of the type of events being investigated, rather than the success or lack of success in getting results by the methods of natural science.

While Hempel is right to point out that "reliance on . . . subjective 'understanding' provides no warrant of objective validity," it does not follow that "warrants of objective validity" in social-scientific contexts can altogether forego any reference to "the interpretation of action in terms of its subjective meaning." If such a reference is indeed presupposed by one widely accepted concept of a social science, as Weber suggests, then the methods of that science must be adapted to its goals. Hence, while Weber's view does amount to "an *a priori* judgment on the character of any set of concepts which can possibly yield explanatory sociological theories," this judgment is by no means "capricious" or "indefensible." For "the concept of a *social* science" which is in question is one which deliberately and explicitly concerns itself with the investigation and explanation of social action or meaningful behavior.

If indeed it is possible to formulate "explanatory principles for purposive action in purely behavioristic . . . terms" (in the sense of an operationalistic, physicalistic "behaviorism"), then social investigators may prefer the Hempelian conception of social science to Weber's conception. But Hempel's claim that "the more recent development of psychological and social theory" *shows* that it is possible to "formulate explanatory principles for purposive action in purely behavioristic, non-introspective terms," is very difficult to substantiate for any but the simplest cases of purposive action. Indeed, even in the simpler cases, it is doubtful whether the behavioristic use of the term *purposive action* has the *same reference* as our ordinary use of this term, or as this term is ordinarily used in historical or sociological contexts.[10]

Finally, one might well ask whether "*a priori* verdicts" on the "character of any set of concepts which can possibly yield explanatory theories" in social science, can be avoided on *anyone's* analysis of social science. For to attempt to define a branch of science in terms of its subject matter is already to render such a verdict. To assert that *all* explanation in the sciences conforms to the causal, nomological model of natural science, is as much an *a priori* verdict as Max Weber's definition of social action.

In claiming that interpretation is necessary to sociological inquiry, Weber has been accused of confusing the context of discovery with the context of justification.[11] This suggestion, however, is clearly incorrect. Weber may have been wrong in supposing that interpretive hypotheses are necessary in social science, but it is clear that from his point of view such interpretation is relevant to *both* contexts. Statistical evidence, for example, is not *sufficient* in order to justify the acceptance of an interpretive hypothesis. The method of interpretive understanding—of extending to the actions of others the direct understanding we would have of our own behavior in similar circumstances—is also required. While this method is uncertain and highly fallible, it cannot be replaced by a more conclusive procedure. If a particular interpretation fails, it can only be replaced by a better interpretation, not by something different in kind.

IV

The Nature
of Societal Knowledge

Can There Be a Natural Science of Society?

One way of understanding Weber is to suppose that while he is attempting to provide the necessary conceptual underpinnings for an interpretive social science, he is not assuming that his approach to the task of constructing a social science is the only possible or legitimate one. For example, a sociologist conceivably could be satisfied with explanations of social phenomena that did not "go beyond merely demonstrating functional relationships and uniformities . . ." and did not aim at "the subjective understanding of the actions of the component individuals." A social scientist of this type, therefore, would not have to employ the method of interpretive understanding, but could restrict himself to the methods of physics in his investigations of social phenomena. True, according to Weber, he would necessarily miss something important, namely, *adequate* causal understanding of social phenomena in terms of motives or meaningful idea types. But it does not follow that a social science which limited itself to the methods of natural science is logically impossible.

According to an argument recently advanced by Peter Winch, however, the idea of a social science in the sense of a natural science of society, is a contradiction in terms, a logical impossibility.[1] In Winch's view, "the conceptions according to which we normally think of social events enter into social life itself and not merely into the observer's description of it" (p. 95). So far Winch would agree with Max Weber. Knowledge gathered merely by a process of sensory observation or inference from data of sensory observation alone, is insufficient for sociological purposes. The sociologist must be concerned with people's actions and social practices, but these items are not presented to the senses of an observer. All that is presented to the senses are certain movements and sounds. What the sociologist is interested in must be described in terms of notions like beliefs, attitudes, expectations, participant ideas, and so on. Hence sociological knowledge involves, in addition to sensory observation, a process of interpretive understanding, i.e., a process of interpreting observed events in the light of the social or institutional context in which they occur.

But Winch seems to go beyond Weber when he says that the conceptions according to which we normally think of social events and that enter into social life itself, are "logically incompatible with the concepts belonging to scientific investigation" (p. 95). By *scientific investigation,* Winch means investigations for which the methods of concept formation, theory construction, and experimental testing employed in the natural sciences are appropriate. Weber never goes quite this far; for Weber, methods of natural science can never be sufficient to accomplish the task of interpretive sociology. But Weber never implies that these methods are logically incompatible with the methods of interpretive sociology, nor that the social scientist can dispense with them where they are applicable, as in *verifying* an interpretive hypothesis or providing a causal explanation of a course of social action.

According to Winch, however, to describe social phenomena in terms of notions like "people holding certain theories" or "believing in certain propositions," is already to have taken the decision to apply a set of concepts "incompatible with the 'external', 'experimental' point of view." To refuse to describe social phenomena in such terms, on the other hand, involves not treating it as having human or *social* significance. It follows, according to Winch, "that the understanding of society cannot be observational and experimental in one widely accepted sense" (p. 95) .

The sense in which Winch is denying that our understanding of society can be observational and experimental is Hume's. It will be recalled that according to Hume, our understanding of logic and mathematics is logically different from our understanding of causal relations and matters of fact. The former concerns itself with internal relations of ideas, while the latter is concerned with external relations of events. The grounds for this distinction are summarized by Hume in a familiar passage from the *Enquiry Concerning Human Understanding:* [2]

> All the objects of human reason or inquiry may naturally be divided into two kinds, to wit, "Relations of Ideas," and "Matters of Fact." Of the first kind are the sciences of Geometry, Algebra, and Arithmetic, and, in short, every affirmation which is either intuitively or demonstratively certain. . . . Propositions of this kind are discoverable by the mere operation of thought, without dependence on what is anywhere existent in the universe. Though there never were a circle or triangle in nature, the truths demonstrated by Euclid would forever retain their certainty and evidence.
>
> Matters of fact, which are the second objects of human reason, are not ascertained in the same manner, nor is our evidence of their truth, however great, of a like nature with the foregoing. The contrary of every matter of fact is still possible, because it can never imply a contradiction and is conceived by the mind with the same facility and distinctness as if ever so conformable to reality. *That the sun will not rise tomorrow* is no less intelligible a proposition and implies no more contradiction than the affirmation *that it will rise.* We should in vain, therefore, attempt to demonstrate its falsehood. Were it demonstratively false, it would

imply a contradiction and could never be distinctly conceived by the mind (Section IV).

According to Hume, since human actions and the events of history are matters of fact, our understanding of them must be observational and experimental, or the same as our understanding of physical events and processes. Hume tried to prove this thesis by showing that in neither kind of case, i.e., neither in the case of human actions nor in the case of physical events, do we have any *idea* of *real connections* of matters of fact.

Winch presumably agrees with Hume as far as our understanding of nature goes, but disagrees with him regarding our understanding of human actions. In effect, Winch argues that in the case of human social relations, we do have ideas of real connections of matters of fact. This is because to understand something as an action requires reference to the institutional context or the social system in which the action is implicated. It is the character of the social system which determines the individual actions, rather than the physical conditions or antecedents of the events we can observe. Thus, for Winch, the concept of a human action implies a social system. Hume's approach is the reverse. Actions are individually determined from *internal* causes; society may modify their character, of course, but the understanding of society depends on the prior understanding of individual actions.

If Winch's premises were true, would it follow that a natural science of society or history is logically impossible? This conclusion would not follow from the above premises alone. That is, even if we grant that the conceptions according to which we normally think of social events are incompatible with scientific conceptions, and that the former enter into social life and must be understood by the social inquirer, we still cannot validly infer that there cannot be a natural science of society. In order to derive this conclusion, Winch would have to show in addition that a putative experimental science of society could not proceed by disregarding the conceptions according to which we normally think of social events. He would have to show that it could not discount the ideas or conceptions of participants, in the manner suggested by Durkheim, and proceed by introducing its own theoretical concepts defined as referring exclusively to observable behavior and causes not necessarily present to the understanding of the social agents. Winch, of course, is aware of this situation. As he points out, "there is a powerful stream of thought which maintains that the ideas of participants must be discounted . . . ," and he cites Durkheim as an important exponent of this tradition (p. 95). What Winch must do, therefore, if he is to establish his case, is to show that the hypothesis used in proposition (10) cited in chapter III in the section on Durkheim, is correct, namely that ". . . in the nature of the case, we are limited to 'explaining' social life by the notions of those who participate in it. . . ." If Winch can establish this hypothesis, then, if we grant his other premises, we would have to concede that a natural science of society is logically impossible.

One approach to establishing this hypothesis is to try to show that its denial leads to absurdity. This in fact is what Winch does. Thus he says, ". . . the crucial question . . . is how far any sense can be given to Durkheim's idea of 'the manner according to which associated individuals are grouped' *apart* from the 'notions' of . . . individuals. . . ." Winch believes that the required sense cannot be given, because "a man's social relations with his fellows are permeated with his ideas about reality." Indeed, according to Winch, social relations are nothing but expressions of men's ideas about reality. Hence it would be impossible to refer to social relations, or explain men's action in society, without referring to their ideas (p. 24, pp. 121ff.).

If Winch is right, then social relations between men and the relations between their motives and their actions are *internal* in Hume's sense. If societal relations and the relations between motives and actions are *matters of fact,* then Winch's view would contradict Hume's claim that there are no internal relations of *matters of fact.* Winch's procedure implies that in his view Hume's characterization of the dichotomy between *relations of ideas* and *matters of fact* is not exhaustive, since he (Winch) holds that "the social relations between men and the ideas which men's actions embody are really the same thing considered from different points of view" (p. 121). In other words, if there are social relations which are nothing but relations of ideas, and if all social relations are matters of fact, then some matters of fact are relations of ideas. When Hume speaks of internal relations, he means relations which are internal to the ideas being considered; but he also assumes that such relations can exist only internally, or in the mind. Winch, however, rejects the whole distinction between the internal and external worlds, or between psychological events which exist only in the mind and physical events which exist independently of the mind. For Winch, unlike Hume, *ideas* are not private mental entities which exist only in the consciousness of each individual, but *concepts* that can exist only in public languages, and languages are a *form of life* that presupposes social relations between men.[3] It follows that the criterion of an internal relation is not a psychological one; it must be *grammatical* and relate to "what it makes sense to say." The grammatical conditions of the possibility of making sense in speaking and writing a language, are the source of internal relations.

Winch admits that identifying social relations with the relations of ideas in a particular social system conflicts with Hume's principle: "There is no object, which implies the existence of any other if we consider these objects in themselves, and never look beyond the ideas we form of them." [4] "There is no doubt," Winch observes, "that Hume intended this to apply to human actions and social life as well as to the phenomena of nature." Winch gives the following argument against accepting this principle of the external relations of all matters of fact.

> ... Hume's principle is not unqualifiedly true even of our knowledge of natural phenomena. If I hear a sound and recognize it as a clap of thunder, I already commit myself to believing in the occurrence of a number of other events —e.g., electrical discharges in the atmosphere—even in calling what I have heard 'thunder'. That is, from 'the idea which I have formed' of what I heard I can legitimately infer 'the existence of other objects'.... To say this, of course, is not to reintroduce any mysterious causal nexus *in rebus,* of a sort to which Hume could legitimately object. It is simply to point out that Hume overlooked the fact that 'the idea we form of an object' does not just consist of elements drawn from our observation of that object in isolation, but includes the idea of connections between it and other objects. . . (p. 124).

This argument raises a question about how we individuate our ideas, or distinguish one from another, and from their mutual relations. Winch's view is evidently that every individual idea is implicated in a system of ideas, so that to conceive of an object is already to conceive of it as connected with other objects.

Winch's argument seems to confuse two cases that Hume keeps distinct. Although Hume assumes that every simple idea is a "distinct existent," i.e., exists separately from every other simple idea, he does not deny that there are *complex* ideas whose relations are internal, e.g., "The sum of the interior angles of a triangle is equal to two right ones." The ideas in a complex idea are thus conceived of as having connections with each other.

With respect to the relations of simple ideas, or different complex ideas, Hume holds only that the relations between these ideas is external and derived from experience, i.e., that these ideas *can* be conceived apart. Thus Hume would not want to deny the legitimacy of the inference from the idea of thunder to the idea of lightning. His point is that we could never arrive at the idea of "electrical discharges in the atmosphere" merely by examining or analyzing our idea of thunder, as we *can* arrive at the idea of a relationship of equality between two right angles and the sum of the interior angles of a triangle merely by examining our idea of a triangle.

Thus Hume distinguishes between the case in which we accept a *theory* according to which thunder is invariably preceded by lightning, and lightning consists of electrical discharges in the atmosphere; and the case in which the idea of X may be said to imply the idea of Y. The idea of thunder does not logically imply the idea of lightning as preceding and causing it. By contrast, the idea of a triangle does imply the idea of a figure with three interior angles. The latter are internally, the former are externally related.

Consequently, if we can infer the existence of lightning from the experience of hearing thunder, it is only because, according to Hume, we accept a theory according to which the former causes the latter, and this theory is empirical, i.e., it concerns invariable *external* relations. Thus Winch's first argument does not provide a refutation of Hume's principle that there is no "object" which "implies the existence of any other if we consider these objects in themselves. . . ."

Nevertheless, let us examine Winch's argument as applied exclusively to social events.

> Consider now a very simple paradigm case of a relation between actions in a human society: that between an act of command and an act of obedience to that command. A sergeant calls 'Eyes right!' and his men all turn their eyes to the right. Now, in describing the men's act in terms of the notion of obedience to a command, one is of course committing oneself to saying that a command has been issued. So far the situation looks precisely parallel to the relation between thunder and electrical storms. But now one needs to draw a distinction. An event's character as an act of obedience is *intrinsic* to it in a way which is not true of an event's character as a clap of thunder; and this is in general true of human acts as opposed to natural events (p. 125).

By saying that "an event's character as an act of obedience is *intrinsic* to it in a way which is not true of an event's character as a clap of thunder," let us suppose Winch means something like the following. The act A is truly described as an "act of obedience" if and only if the agent who performs the act understands what he is doing as an act of obedience. It follows that we could not describe the event as an act of obedience unless it contained, as an ingredient in the event itself, the idea or concept of *obeying a command*. But of course it is not true that an event described as a clap of thunder contains the idea or concept of *thunder*. Hence the former event is *meaningful* in Weber's sense while the latter is merely a *natural* event.

Even so, we cannot validly infer from the occurrence of an act of obedience that a command has actually been issued, i.e., that there *exists* (or did exist) an act of command. At most, all that we would be entitled to infer is that the agent *believes* that a command has been issued. But an agent's belief may be false. So there is still no case for saying that there can be an internal relation between two distinct events, such that we can infer the existence of one from that of the other. And this was all that Hume was concerned to establish. Thus Winch's arguments do not refute Hume's principle. The fact that "in describing the men's act in terms of the notion of obedience to a command, one is . . . committing oneself to saying that a command has been issued," does *not* imply that a command has been issued, anymore than describing an object as a unicorn implies that a unicorn exists.

In another passage, Winch says:

> . . . it does not make sense to suppose that human beings might have been issuing commands and obeying them before they came to form the concept of command and obedience. For their performance of such acts is itself the chief manifestation of their possession of those concepts. An act of obedience itself contains, as an essential element, a recognition of what went before as an order. But

> it would of course be senseless to suppose that a clap of
> thunder contained any recognition of what went before
> as an electrical storm; it is our recognition of the sound,
> rather than the sound itself, which contains that recogni-
> tion of what went before (p. 125).

In this passage, Winch claims that an act of obedience contains, as an essential element, a recognition of what went
before as an order. Now if *recognition* means having a *true
belief* that what went before was an order, then of course it
follows logically from the premise that there was such an
act of recognition that there existed an order or command.
But it would not be true, generally speaking, that we cannot perform acts of obedience without recognizing what
went before as an order. For we could sincerely perform an
act of obedience in the belief that an order was issued, when
that belief was false. Perhaps what the sergeant said was
not "Eyes right!" but "I'm right!"

On the other hand, it is true, as a matter of fact, that
if the human practice of issuing commands had never existed, the human practice of performing acts of obedience to
commands would never have existed. So, generally speaking,
there *is* an internal relation between the *idea* of obeying
a command and the *idea* of commanding. This conclusion,
however, is entirely consistent with Hume's principle that
all internal relations are *internal to the mind* or exist only
in the *understanding*.

However, Winch's claim that the performance of acts
such as commanding or obeying is the chief manifestation
of the agent's possession of those concepts, does not imply
that it *makes no sense* to suppose that human beings might
have been issuing commands and obeying them before they
came to form the concept of command and obedience. This
would be like saying that people could not have spoken a
language correctly before they came to form the concept of
a *grammar*. The most that Winch is entitled to say here is
that the actions of issuing commands and obeying, and other
similar behavior, imply that the agents are *capable* of

forming the relevant concepts; and that the fact that people often or usually are in possession of such concepts when they behave in the appropriate ways, differentiates their actions from natural events such as a clap of thunder, in such a way that explanations of the former must differ from explanations of the latter. But this conclusion, which we will investigate in the next chapter, does not go beyond Max Weber.

When Winch says that in the case of natural events, ". . . although human beings can think of the occurrences in question only in terms of the concepts they do in fact have of them, yet the events themselves have an existence independent of those concepts," he suggests that social events, by contrast, do *not* have any existence independent of the concepts in terms of which human beings do in fact think of them. If so, the concept of a social event and the event itself, such as an act of obedience, would be internally related. Now for the reasons stated above, this does not seem to be true in general. Yet it might be true of *some* social events; i.e., there might be some social events such that the event could not have occurred unless the agent possessed the requisite concept. For example, the act of adding up a column of figures seems to be impossible unless the person performing the act possesses the relevant concepts of arithmetic. This fact about social events seems to imply a genuine difference between social events of that type and all natural events. Once again, however, this conclusion does not go beyond Weber. Thus when Weber says that in " 'action' is included all human behavior when and in so far as the acting individual attaches a subjective meaning to it," he seems to have just such a point in mind. It is in virtue of the internal relation between the agent's *understanding* of his action and that action itself, that Weber is led to his conclusion that interpretive understanding is a necessary feature of empirical sociology.

To sum up this discussion, Winch's case for saying that the understanding of society is logically different from the understanding of nature rests on his claim that social events are *internally related,* unlike natural events. Our examination of Winch's arguments has revealed an important ambiguity in this thesis. In the case of social events of the type Weber calls social action, there *is* an internal relation between the agent's action and his understanding of that action. But we cannot infer from the existence of such a relation that the agent's understanding of his action is a true or adequate understanding of the events surrounding his action. In particular, we cannot infer that because the agent believes that he was motivated to act by a certain event, such as the event of someone else issuing a command, that the event did indeed happen. Thus Winch's claim that social *events* are internally related in such a way that the existence of one social event implies the existence of another, does not follow. Hume's principle that "there is no object [i.e., no event] that implies the existence of any other, if we consider those objects in themselves. . . ." appears to apply to distinct social events as well as to physical events.

On the other hand, the premise that there is an internal relation between the agent's action and his understanding of that action, in cases of intentional human actions, seems to imply that the ideas of participants cannot be disregarded by a social science which aims to explain intentional human activity. And this conclusion would be sufficient to refute Durkheim's contention that participant ideas *must* be disregarded by history and sociology. Consequently, if one accepts Durkheim's claim that disregarding participant ideas is a necessary condition of a social science, then one must conclude that there cannot be a social science. Alternatively, one can conclude that Durkheim was mistaken in contending that a necessary condition of a social science is that it disregard participant ideas. In either case, the unity of method thesis is in jeopardy. If we take into account participant ideas in framing our explanations of their behavior, then we are led to say that the social sciences must employ a method of interpretive understanding which has no parallel in the natural sciences. If we refuse to take into account participant ideas, we are led to say that there are kinds of events—namely those consisting in intentional human actions—which cannot be investigated adequately by methods of natural science.

Collingwood's Historical Method

Winch's view of social science has much in common with the philosophy of history of a British historian and philosopher, R. G. Collingwood (1889–1943).[5] According to Collingwood, all characteristically human experience involves thinking, and the actions of men are inseparable from the thoughts that these actions express. The fact that social and historical events contain thoughts leads Collingwood to conclude that they cannot be investigated profitably by the methods of natural science. Thoughts do not merely exist as psychological events; they also have the property of being true or false, consistent or inconsistent. One who investigates experiences or actions which involve thoughts, with the aim of saying something relevant about them, must first master their intellectual content. This would apply especially, for example, to the sociologist or psychologist of religion, since a religion is a system of thoughts or beliefs. The sociologist need not evaluate the truth or falsehood of a system of religious beliefs, but he cannot treat them, or the behavior to which they give rise, as if their property of truth or falsehood made no difference to his investigation. But the method of mastering a system of thought requires a critical study of it from the standpoint of its logical consistency, its internal coherence, and its plausibility in the sense of potential matter of belief for a rational being.

Similarly, explanations of human actions, to be adequate, must take account of the background of thought which may lie behind them. Thus studies of human societies and actions must, to be adequate, take the form of an *intellectual history* or *criticism*. Hence a social scientist, in relation to his subject matter, is not in the same position as a physical scientist in relation to the subject matter of physics. The social scientist is rather in a position like that of a physical scientist who is studying scientific theories, attempting to understand them. The physical scientist must first master the intellectual content of those theories before he can test their relative acceptability by scientific method. But it is not those *theories* that constitute the subject matter of a physical or natural science—rather, the subject matter of a physical science is what those theories are supposed to be *about,* or to be true of. Just as a physical scientist cannot use scientific method in order to understand the content of rival theories, so a social scientist cannot use scientific method in order to understand the intellectual content—the way of life—of a rival social system, or a type of human experience involving reflective thought, such as religious experience. Scientific method only enters the picture when our aim is to adjudicate the truth or falsehood of rival social theories, which are not about systems of thought.

The distinctive method of investigation the social scientist must use, according to Collingwood, is the "historical method" of critically evaluating sources. Furthermore, according to Collingwood, in so far as human actions and experiences involve thoughts, they can only be explained by the *historical method,* i.e., only by reenacting the sequence of thoughts which led the historical agent to perform his action. This view fits in well with Weber's account of the method of sociology, and enables us to see the necessity, for this point of view, of *ideal-type* explanations for explaining the development of social or group action. There is no single sequence of thoughts to be reenacted in the case of the history of a social institution, for example; but the thinking of the various individuals whose actions created the institution can be typified and idealized in a way that gives an accurate understanding of the nature of the changes and why they occurred.

Is Societal Knowledge Empirical?

A follower of Hume and Mill would claim that even if it is true that men's ideas about their behavior enter into social life itself, and that the social sciences must therefore be in part a study of men's ideas and their relations, there is still no reason why we cannot have an empirical or natural science of social life. They would support this thesis by pointing out that hypotheses in the social studies must be tested by comparison with facts that are not knowable *a priori* but only by experience and observation. So even if our conceptions of men's social relations and practices are not founded on observations in the same way as our conceptions of physical relations and events, the knowledge-claims from which these conceptions are formulated must be subjected to empirical testing in the same way as hypotheses in the natural sciences.

To this, an interpretationist might reply that the term *empirical* is ambiguous in respect to social and physical contexts, or as it applies to the social sciences, on the one hand, and natural or physical sciences on the other. If all that is meant by *empirical* is that we have no knowledge of men's social practices independently of experience, then we may agree that our knowledge of society is empirical. But it does not follow that the same species of observation that is employed in making empirical discoveries in the natural sciences can be employed in the social sciences, nor that discoveries in the social sciences can be evaluated by the same kind of criteria that are employed in evaluating physical hypotheses. Thus, if by *empirical knowledge* is meant knowledge derived from data of sensory observation alone, then our knowledge of society is not illuminatingly described as *empirical*, since the latter kind of knowledge involves, in addition to sensory observation, the process of understanding a language and of interpreting sensory data in the light of the social or institutional context in which it occurs.

This interpretationist view is not refuted merely by showing that statistical methods of measurement and behavioristic methods of experimenting can be adapted to sociological contexts. For it may still be the case that in order to make such adaptations successfully or fruitfully, we must take into account the logical differentia whereby we distinguish social events from mere physical processes. The assumption that social events can profitably be investigated by methods of natural science, in other words, does not relieve us of the obligation of having to state the characteristics that an event must have in order to qualify for membership in the class of *social* events. For if we cannot state these requirements, then we cannot say what it is to observe *social* events as opposed to observing occurrences at random. Thus the use of statistical and behavioristic methods in social inquiries, even so far as they are successful or fruitful, does not entail that there are no differences in principle between the methods of the social and physical sciences.

The question whether such differences in principle exist depends not on what specific methods of research are employed by a social scientist, but on the nature of the *explanatory principles* that he must presuppose in order to justify his claim that he is investigating a social subject matter. The nature of these explanatory principles will be determined, presumably, not merely by the bias of the investigator, but by the nature of the societal facts and the conditions which make it possible for us to understand these facts. Thus the supplementary use of statistical and behavioristic methods in the social sciences is entirely compatible with the thesis that the social sciences must employ, in addition to the usual methods of scientific observation and testing, a method of interpretive understanding. Furthermore, there is nothing in the development of contemporary social or psychological theory which contradicts this claim; for after all statistical and behavioristic methods have been applied, it may still remain a task for the social investigator to connect his *quantitative* results to a social subject matter, in order to arrive at an explanation of the specifically social aspect of the phenomena.

On the other hand, the assumption that the explanatory principles utilized in the social sciences are logically distinct from the explanatory principles utilized in natural science, does not entail that all uses of quantitative methods, or of *causal-theoretic* forms of explanation, are superfluous or objectionable. In fact, as Max Weber recognized and pointed out, an interpretive explanation in social science or history must also be causally adequate. Furthermore, there can be no good reason for restricting or inhibiting research by any available means.

If so, the important question regarding the nature of our knowledge of society is not whether it is empirical, nor whether statistical, behavioristic, or causal-theoretic methods are ever appropriate to social inquiry, but what is the nature of the observational base of social studies and how, if at all, it differs from the observational base presupposed by natural scientific investigation. This question is important because the way we answer it will influence our conception of the subject matter of social inquiry, as well as our view of what constitutes a *satisfactory* explanation in social science.

Social Events.

In order to make this clearer, let us begin by examining what is involved in ordinary observation of events in which human verbal behavior plays a part, as opposed to observing an event that does not involve social action of any kind. I shall call the former kind of event a *social event* and the latter kind a *physical event*. By this I do not mean that all social events involve a verbal component, but merely that any event which involves a verbal component, in the sense of a meaningful use of language, can be classified as social. By *meaningful use of language*, I wish to exclude nonsense and parroting of syllables. In other words, the sense of *verbal* in which I am interested is the same as that in which psychologists and sociologists speak of gathering data on the basis of *verbal reports*. Such data are also indispensable to other social sciences. A verbal report, in this sense, is an interaction between persons in society, and hence necessarily a social event.

In order to compare what is involved in observing a social event of this kind with what is involved in observing a physical event, let us take the Galilean experiment of the fall of two physical objects of unequal weight through the atmosphere as a paradigm of something that we can observe in the sense of observation of a physical event. On the other hand, let us consider the performance of a mathematician lecturing in a classroom as a paradigm of what we can observe in the *social* sense of observation. In the case of the performing mathematician, the problem for the social investigator is to observe what the mathematician is doing, in the same way that he would observe the fall of two bodies. This is a fair example, since for any ordinary human observer there is nothing more difficult about the former case than the latter, assuming that the mathematician speaks the same language as the observer. It would be pointless to compare the observation of the mathematician's performance to a complex physical experiment requiring complicated equipment and theories, which only a comparatively few scientists are capable of understanding.

In comparing the observation of the mathematician's activity with the event of the falling bodies, the first thing to notice is that *it makes sense* to distinguish between a description of the mathematician's *physical* motions, and a description of *what he is doing* in the ordinary sense of those words, viz., giving a lecture; while *it makes no sense whatever* to suggest such a distinction in the case of the falling bodies. That is to say, a total physical description of the mathematician's arm-waving, the chalk he flings about the room, the sounds emanating from his lips, the physical path of his body in relation to the room, the muscular disturbances going on throughout his body, his nervous system and brain processes, would not be sufficient in order to convey to someone *what he is doing.* In order to complete the description, we would have to describe, not just the sounds he is emitting and the motions of his body, internal and external, but also the *words* and *sentences* conveyed by those sounds. Obviously the words and sentences are not identifiable with any particular physical activity of the mathematician, since the same words and sentences can be conveyed by different physical media, e.g., vocal emissions of a wide range and variety, gestures, written inscriptions, facial expressions, etc. But how do we observe *words* and *sentences,* as opposed to hearing sounds and seeing gestures and inscriptions?

A precondition of *observing* words and sentences, as opposed to hearing mere sounds and seeing mere marks, i.e., of *observing* what someone is saying, is not only that the observer understand what it is to speak a language, but more basically that he be able to identify the relevant *sign vehicles* of the language being used. There is no need to suppose that anything mysterious or occult is involved in the ability to understand a language; it is merely necessary to grasp that the case of observing a social event differs from the case of observing a physical event, in that the former involves understanding a language as a precondition of making the observation. We need not suppose that social observation involves two distinct processes: one rather straightforward process called *empirical observation* and hidden beneath that an occult process called *understanding a language.* The point is merely that the social observer must be able to distinguish between a case of language behavior and a mere physical occurrence, *before* he can make a relevant social observation. Otherwise, the social observer would have no reason to attach any more significance to the sounds emanating from the mathematician's lips than he does to the mathematician's arm-waving and chalk-flinging.

But what is involved in being able to make such a distinction as that between a series of sounds or marks and a meaningful use of language? That is to say, what is involved in being able to understand a language?

Suppose that we were explorers visiting another planet where we encountered a species of intelligent life physiologically quite unlike any with which we are familiar on earth, and we wished to discover the manner of communication of these creatures. Let us imagine that the degree of complexity of their behavior and the novelty of their responses makes it likely that they communicate in some fashion. We can also suppose that they accompany their actions with the emission of complex noise patterns similar to the sort of thing we do when we speak.

At first we might believe that these creatures communicate by sounds much as we do, but suppose that after numerous unsuccessful attempts to communicate with them by means of speech, we eventually conclude that the noises these creatures make do not serve the communicative function that sound emission often does in human beings. We would come to this conclusion if we experimented and found, for example, that interrupting the transmission of their noises did not alter their responses in any relevant respect. Thus we might insert a sound-proof but transparent partition between two of them as they seemed to be "talking," and observe that they are apparently insensible of any interruption.

Let us suppose, however, that as we observe these creatures pursuing their activities, their physical gestures and the sounds they emit often remind us very forcibly of the behavior of a distracted mathematician lecturing in a classroom. In such a situation, the physical description of these creatures' activities could be analogous to a description of a human mathematician lecturing in a classroom; yet this description would not be an index to the manner of communication of these creatures. Whatever observations we could make of their physical behavior would be of no use, in the imagined circumstances, for testing claims about their social practices and institutions, so far as a knowledge of the latter depended upon an understanding of their language.

Nevertheless, we might still be able to measure the responses of their organisms to stimuli, in the same way that we measure such responses in human organisms. That is, we could conceivably measure any change in external energy which excited receptor cells in their bodies, causing neural activity that eventually resulted in some objectively measurable response. We might also be able to measure highly complex patterns of muscular movements, such as those occurring when a human subject speaks a word. And we might be able to give reports that described their responses in terms of physical dimensions such as time, speed, magnitude, and probability of occurrence. We might be able to do all this, and yet be unable to describe their manner of communication or form any testable hypothesis about the items of their behavior which function as sign vehicles or elements of a language. Let us suppose, however, that in the course of our investigations, we discover that there are certain differences in the physiological structure of these creatures' bodies, in their brains and nervous systems, which distinguish them from human beings, but which we are unable to account for.

Suppose that while conducting these experiments we join with these creatures as often as possible in their daily pursuits, which are mainly agricultural, and which require them to make long excursions from their "villages." One day we observe that one of the extra-terrestrial creatures has an "accident." We observe, furthermore, that although the other creatures in the vicinity attempt to relieve the victim's immediate discomfort, they make no effort to return to their homes or to send for aid. Nevertheless, within a short time, assistance does arrive, and the stricken individual is carried away.

In this situation, the hypothesis that would suggest itself is that these creatures are so constituted physiologically as to be able to achieve, between themselves, direct soundless communication, even over long distances. Confronted with these circumstances, we make the hypothesis that these creatures are able to control radio waves, but without having to employ special mechanical devices in order to receive and transmit such waves. Now let us suppose that this hypothesis is tested and corroborated; and that we are eventually able to achieve communication with these creatures by employing the radio equipment on our spaceship. At this point, fruitful empirical study of the social institutions of our extra-terrestrial creatures can begin.

Of course these imaginary examples are highly improbable. It is highly unlikely that we would ever encounter a species of life capable of communicating in the way imagined, much less one that also appeared to speak as we do. But the example is not inconceivable. Perhaps noise emission in these creatures would be a side effect of their radio transmissions, of one of which they have ceased to be much aware because of its familiarity. In any case, the fact that it is possible to imagine a community of this sort illustrates the point that observation and the adequate description of social behavior presupposes the capacity to understand what it is to have a language. It also shows that in order for us to discover the manner of communication of a species of intelligent life, the relevant sign vehicles or the media of meaning must be physiologically accessible to us. But more important than the above, our example shows that having a language may not be connected by a law of nature with a particular type or range of macroscopic physical events or bodily functions, such as the emission of sounds or bodily gestures. The connection between having a language and exercising a particular bodily function, in other words, may be only a *conventional* con-

nection, which could vary widely and unpredictably between one form of biological life and another. If so, we
would have to discover the relevant conventions *before* we
could discover the sign vehicles or the language. Hence,
before we could identify an event as a case of social or
meaningful behavior, we would have to establish that an
intended meaning or *sense* is being associated by the agent
with the particular instance of behavior, although this asso-
ciation need not consist in a particular mental act or
conscious judgment.

Two factors of importance emerge from this consideration. One is that the ability to make sensory observations
is not sufficient to enable us to form relevant hypotheses
as to which events among those observed involve a linguistic
or meaningful component. The other is that in order to
test hypotheses about intended meanings and the social
institutions which depend on there being a community of
such meanings, it is not sufficient to refer to what we can
observe in sensory observation alone. In other words, if
we use *verbal reports* to test a sociological or psychological
hypothesis, then those reports are not merely observational
reports but are *translational hypotheses* themselves. The
logical problems involved in testing or verifying translational hypotheses will be investigated in the eighth chapter.

The only point we need to make at present is that understanding a language is often necessary in order to discriminate a social event, and that hypotheses about such social
events can often be tested only by reference to the translational hypotheses being assumed for the purposes of testing.
Hence understanding a language is necessary not only to the
discrimination of the events being described, but also in
order to justify explanatory hypotheses about such events.
Understanding a language may also be necessary in order
to discriminate some *physical* events, at least in ways that
would be useful for science. But there is an additional involvement of language in describing social events. This
additional involvement is that the social events, as in our

example, may be partly *constituted* by language. Consequently, a social description involving description of what agents mean by their words must be conditioned by the linguistic framework or conceptual system involved in the behavior being described. This is a factor in social description that has no correspondence in descriptions of physical events. Although the physical motions involved in a social practice of an alien society might resemble certain physical motions with which we are familiar in our own practice, they might take on an entirely different significance for the alien society, or even be devoid of significance altogether. Thus suppose that we wish to describe a social practice of our newly discovered extra-terrestrial society. Our description, if it is to serve as part of an explanation of the relevant behavior, must take into account the extra-terrestrial's standards for saying when a particular occurrence is to be understood as a case of that practice.

In the physical sciences, there is nothing comparable to this need to take into account the standards of others. In giving a physical explanation, we must take into account only what is believed or disbelieved, intelligible or unintelligible, by *our* standards and social practices, or by scientific standards. But in attempting to explain the practices of an alien society, we have to consider as well the alien creature's standards of intelligibility and unintelligibility. This consideration brings out the fact that the way people conceptualize their behavior forms an essential part of the subject matter of social science, whereas in the physical sciences conceptualizations belong exclusively to the theorizer or scientist. The natural scientist employs a concept of gravity which he introduces in giving physical explanations of events, but he is not engaged in explaining the concept of having a concept of gravity, in giving such an explanation.

The social scientist, however, who is engaged in explaining a particular social event at the level of language, not only *uses* the concept of the event in his explanation; he also mentions it and may even have to explain the meaning of the concept before he can explain the relevant behavior. If this is so, it follows that the criteria of successful social explanation of meaningful behavior cannot be the same as the criteria of a successful physical explanation, since in general the *explanation* of conceptual interconnections is very different from the causal model of explanation employed in the natural sciences. We shall try to show in what respects the former kind of explanation differs from the latter in the subsequent section of this chapter and in chapter V.

Societal Explanation.

An interesting example of how historico-sociological explanations involve interpretive understanding and the mention of the concepts used in giving the explanation is the following. In his Introduction to his edition of Hume's *Dialogues Concerning Natural Religion,* Norman Kemp Smith wants to explain how Hume's philosophical views developed out of the social and intellectual climate of the eighteenth-century Scottish view of human life.[6]

> In Hume's early years, the religion which prevailed in Scotland, with hardly even the suggestion of a serious rival, was of a highly specific type, extreme in its own kind, and quite the least suited, either by its doctrines or by its prescribed modes of life, to enlighten him regarding the limitations of his own contrary outlook. It was a popularized version of Calvin's teaching, retaining its darker features, and representing even these in a distorted and exaggerated form. . . . A harsh and unlovely type of poverty was the common fate; even among the upper class it was but little tempered by more gracious ways of life. Methods of agriculture were so primitive that even a single bad harvest brought famine and widespread mendicancy in its train. . . . In the provincial towns such little trade as there had been was stagnant, and the population was declining. Edinburgh, the only town of any size, was losing its nobility and some of its most distinguished commoners to London. With so little to encourage the country to hopeful

initiative, and so much to fill it with despair and gloom, it is not surprising that in the years preceding and following the Union [i.e., the union of the Parliaments in 1707] the temper of the people should have reacted upon the life of the Church, and that its Calvinist teaching, always grimly austere, should have become even·more bleak and gloomy, and that many old-time superstitions and fanaticisms should have gained a new lease of life. . . .

Kemp Smith, to enforce his explanation of how Scottish conditions influenced Hume's view of religion, cites another historian, writing about the same period of Scottish history.[7]

During the seventeenth century Scottish religion had fallen under the influence of English Puritanism; and when to this we add the memory of the bitter strife of sixty years, and the economic misery of the moment, we can perhaps understand why at the Union, and for many years after, religion was seen in its grimmest form. . . . [It] depicted God as an implacable despot, swift to wrath. . . . It held by the doctrines of election and reprobation in all their severity. . . . Both in church and in home the most relentless discipline was maintained. . . . The observance of the Sabbath was enforced with penalties. All other sacred times and seasons were deliberately ignored.

If one examines these passages impartially, it is difficult to deny (1) that they are explanatory, (2) that they provide us with knowledge (3) that this knowledge is empirically based and (4) that it essentially involves the *mention* as well as the *use* of the concepts possessed by the Scots at the time being described. If one deletes from these passages such subjective elements as "religion was seen in its grimmest form," "harsh and unlovely type of poverty," and so on, one deprives the explanation of its explanatory force and sense. If, on the other hand, one accepts the view that these explanations have force and that they essentially involve the mention of concepts or ideas of participants, but denies that they are *scientific,* then one is agreeing with Durkheim and Winch that only explanations of the causal-theoretic type, involving no reference to participant ideas, ought to be admitted as scientific. This, however, is merely a verbal point, unless it can be shown that interpretive explanations involve untestable hypotheses. A person who insists that in so far as these explanations give us knowledge, they can be reconstructed in causal-theoretic form, or in some other standard form of physical explanation, may be insisting on a dogma. In the next chapter, we will consider whether explanations of conceptual interconnections (e.g., the subjective connection between the economic and religious climate of the Scotland of Hume's boyhood) can be represented in terms of external or causal relations of events.

V

Explaining
Human Actions

Causal and Interpretive Explanations.

As we have seen, scientific empiricists such as Hempel hold that purposive actions can be explained by the same principles as natural events. A central difficulty with this view is that assertions of causal connections entail a causal law covering events of the type to be explained, but we often seem to be able to explain purposive actions even when we do not know any appropriate causal laws. On the other hand, Max Weber, an interpretationist, asserts that the social sciences do seek adequate causal understanding of social and human action. We shall try to solve this problem in the present section.

In the social sciences, we sometimes interest ourselves in the reasons that an agent would give for his actions. We then attempt to explain his actions by citing his reasons. Following Weber, we shall call explanations of this type *interpretive*. They differ in interesting ways, as we shall see, from standard causal explanations as analyzed by Hume, Hempel, and other logical empiricists.

What distinguishes an interpretive explanation is that it involves explaining behavior by reference to the agent's conceptions of what he is doing, as opposed to explaining it by causal laws. Interpretive explanation takes into account the fact that an agent's knowledge of his own actions differs in important ways from that which an observer can have of those actions. This characteristic is included in the notion of an interpretive explanation, since the acceptability of the latter is determined, in part, by the agent's testimony (in standard cases). There is no reason why both causal and interpretive types of explanations of the same human action should not be possible, but often interpretive explanations are available to us when causal explanations are not. Hence the usefulness of the former for a social science.

Applied to many human actions, an interpretive explanation connects features of what the agent did to features of the social setting in which he acted, and his desires, goals, or thoughts, as these would ordinarily be described by the agent or his fellow men. It aims to elucidate the connections between the action and its conditions as envisaged, e.g., by the agent, and is explanatory only if the descriptions it sets forth of the features of the social setting, etc., would not be true unless its description of what the agent did were true. Various interpretive explanations cover what anti-causal theorists see as important for understanding human actions. Yet such accounts neither presuppose nor rule out an explanation which applies causal laws to the same action and the events or circumstances that preceded or accompanied it.

This conclusion concerns a widely recognized but much disputed feature of reasons for action, namely that an agent's knowledge of them is not experimental or observational. Since all other causes are known experimentally, and certified through observation, how can reasons be causes? I shall argue that there is no inconsistency between according a privileged status to an agent's report of why he acted, and counting his reasons among the causes of his deed. No contradiction arises, because the agent's description of these causal factors may very well differ from the description of them which appears in a relevant causal law; and such a law forms the backbone of any fullfledged causal explanation of what the agent did. In other words, the agent may not know the cause of his action as this cause would be specified in a scientist's account of his deed.

In the case of human actions, we are often baffled precisely because we lack an interpretive account of someone's
deeds, and it would not help us to find out that his deeds
exemplified a causal regularity. Travelers in exotic countries experience this puzzlement from time to time. In the
hills of Kabylia, for instance, you notice a group of bedouins
who calmly play flutes, tap drums, and smoke their pipes
while a boy gyrates about, periodically stabbing himself in
the legs and arms. What is up? Is he beserk? Are the by-
standers allowing him to commit suicide? Nothing of the
sort. What you see is a religious ritual, part of a forbidden
animistic cult; the youth is performing a sacred dance.
You might want to hear other salient details of the cult and
this ceremony. And once you have this interpretive explanation of the behavior you witnessed, you might also inquire
about causes. What made the participants engage in this
ritual at this particular time? What historical events and
conditions produced this cult in the first place? But the
causal explanations you would get in reply are entirely
distinct from the original specification you received of what
was going on, and what made it the sort of event it was.

What bearing does this distinction have upon the philosophical wrangle about explaining human behavior? One
source of the dispute is that any item of human behavior,
such as the bedouins' ceremony, may be reported in a variety
of idioms. The alternative vocabularies at our disposal may
not be interchangeable. A report of the behavior in one
idiom is not synonymous with reports of it in another. And
this creates trouble when we get around to explaining it.
Characterized in one set of terms, the behavior is made
intelligible by further statements in the same idiom, but it
becomes no more intelligible than before when the description of it is accompanied by statements in another terminology. Many philosophers mis-diagnose this trouble. They
attribute the difficulty to an irremediable clash between
causal explanation and the other things we find worth
saying about human behavior, rather than to an incongruity

between the expressions we use to report the behavior, and the expressions we use in explaining it.

Here is an illustration of how multiple descriptions for the same item of behavior create trouble. It demonstrates why the philosophical diagnosis of the trouble is incorrect. The scene of action is a Florida beach; a number of vacationers are basking in the sun, some are afloat in the surf, and a lifeguard is on top of his watchtower. A bather goes under, and the action begins: the lifeguard dashes into the water and hauls the bather to safety. So far, our rudimentary narrative is in the everyday language of gross material objects and human activity. But you could set forth the very same event without these terms. You might single out the event, and enable your listeners to identify it for purposes of further discussion and investigation, if you limited yourself to the vocabulary of physics and physiology. For instance, you might record the geographical location and the posture of certain organisms, the condition of their bones and muscles, the operation of their nervous systems, and the various changes of position, posture, neural activity, and so on, that ensue over this particular stretch of time. An attentive listener could then pinpoint the event you referred to; he would be able to visit the scene and gather more information about the episode, even though you had not uttered words like *bathing beach, lifeguard, swimmer in danger,* and *rescue.*

What would an interpretive explanation of the incident sound like? That depends upon the description of it that you begin with, and your interest in it. If you were a physiologist, no doubt you would start with a report of some bodily motions, and you would demand more details about them, so that it would become clear to you exactly what sorts of bodily processes took place. If you are a newspaper reporter, a lawyer or a sociologist, you would not be satisfied if an eyewitness gave his testimony in physiological terms. Even if you knew physiology, you would want another account of the episode. You would want to hear about its legal, social, moral and emotional aspects.

Suppose you begin with this report: A swimmer was in danger of drowning, and the lifeguard on duty rescued him. For your purposes, an interpretive explanation of the event, as described thus far, would provide answers to questions from one or more of the following groups:

(1) Concerning the lifeguard:
    (a) What is it to be a lifeguard?
    (b) What tests does one pass to be a lifeguard?
    (c) What does a lifeguard have to do with people who are swimming at the beach where he is stationed?
    (d) What is it to have the duty of saving people?
    (e) By means of what institutions do governments protect people from harm?

(2) Concerning the bather:
    (a) What is it to be on vacation?
    (b) What is it to have the right to be protected from drowning?
    (c) What is drowning?
    (d) By what standards do we judge that a person is in danger of some harm, such as drowning?
    (e) Had the bather himself neglected to take some customary precautions against drowning?

(3) Concerning the action:
    (a) What makes an event an act by one of the participants in the event?
    (b) What features of the lifeguard's performance on this occasion make it the specific act of rescuing?

According to your ignorance of the society in which this incident took place, these and similar inquiries would be worth pursuing. Only 2 (c) could be answered satisfactorily by a witness who limited himself to the terms of physiology. All the other questions in groups (1) and (2) call for interpretive explanations of normative features of the incident. The notions of being a lifeguard, being stationed somewhere, having an obligation towards people, government, danger, harm, safety, and precautions, are normative notions in the straightforward sense that they only apply to things when there is a society with various types of norms. If a number of men are not members of any social group, then it is impossible that one of them should be a lifeguard, an employee of the municipal government, and responsible for the others' safety on a particular beach; nor could another of them neglect safety measures and risk drowning. These relationships, and the lifeguard's action of performing his duty, require a setting of laws, customs, authority, and participation in common activities such as vacationing. It would be mad, therefore, to demand from physiology an interpretive explanation for these aspects of the incident. It follows that a causal explanation, in physiological terms, of the various bodily motions that took place during the rescue will never elucidate its normative features.

But this sketch of an interpretive explanation shows a lot more than a clash between (I) causal explanation of bodily processes, and (II) interpretive explanation of the events that comprised these bodily processes. In fact, (I) and (II) are not really incompatible. How could they be, since they are both correct explanations of the same event? (I) will not do the same job as (II), and conversely, but who expects them to replace each other? The point is that (I) and (II) are both explanations of the same incident. Each explains different elements in it, and in a different manner. There would be just as much of a clash, and just as little, between *either* (I) *or* (II) and an interpretive explanation for the bodily processes which figured in the rescue—viz., a physiological account of what sorts of processes these were—as we found *between* (I) and (II).

This latter consequence deserves elaboration. Presumably the bodily processes that occur during the rescue are not human actions. But they resemble actions inasmuch as they may be reported in a variety of idioms, and these reports are not interchangeable. A physiological description of a bodily process is not synonymous with a description of the same process in everyday non-technical language. So with respect to events that are not actions, such as bodily processes, it is also true that a causal explanation will not replace an interpretive explanation of them, and that a particular interpretive explanation is suitable only when the event is described in the same family of terms as the explanation. So it is not a peculiarity of actions that interpretive and causal explanations for them will not stand in for each other. Furthermore, the peculiarity is not just that we cannot substitute a causal for an interpretive account of an action or a bodily movement. Interpretive explanations that are stated in mutually exclusive idioms are just as unsuited to replace each other. For example, if you want to know what gross bodily movements took place during the rescue, and you have no interest in physiological minutiae, then an interpretive explanation in physiological terms would be useless to you.

Returning now to the topic of action, how does this long-winded example help reconcile philosophers who disagree about the possibility of causal explanations for what a person does? All disputants seem to believe that a physiologist could give us a causal explanation of the bodily movements that go into actions like the rescue. Our illustration shows that the physiologist would not thereby give us any kind of explanation—causal or interpretive—for the normative features of the very same event. We outlined an interpretive explanation which brings these features into relief. Finally, the example proves that this interpretive explanation is perfectly compatible with the physiologist's causal account of non-normative elements, and also compatible with any interpretive explanation he might propound for these non-normative elements.

In fact, our illustration proves that an interpretive account of the normative features we see in the rescue cannot block a causal explanation of these very same features. Naturally you would not substitute the causal account for an interpretive explanation; you must understand what the social and institutional background of the rescue is before you explain what caused the background to develop as it did. And presumably such a causal account of the norms that enter into the lifeguard's performance will not be restricted to the official vocabulary of physiology. But otherwise, why rule out causal explanation of these elements *a priori?* Don't historians, anthropologists, sociologists and political scientists already offer some causal accounts of norms? An explanation does not have to be complete and inalterable; it ought merely to provide some new insights into the social conventions we are studying.

So far we have not examined actions that are unconnected with social institutions. Can we also demonstrate that both causal and interpretive explanation apply to them? For convenience, we will prolong our story of the rescue, except that we will now delete the normative background that has been the focus of our interpretive explanation of the incident. At present, that is, we will forget the rescuer's job, his qualifications, his duties, and accepted standards of safety and danger. Is anything left over when we suppress these factors? Can we call our protagonist a rescuer anymore, and his performance a rescue? Yes, if we paint in some fresh background, which is free of institutional overtones. Our story will be amended as follows. Our protagonist is not a lifeguard anymore; he is a noble savage, uncontaminated by society. He comes upon a beach, notices another noble savage drowning, and pulls him to shore. This still sounds like an action—a rescue, in fact—although it is plainly *not* a case of someone carrying out his official duties, keeping others out of danger, or performing a feat of heroism over and above the call of duty.

An interpretive explanation of the occurrence would have to deal with the inquiries we listed in group (3) above. It would thus settle two questions: (a) Why was the incident an action by the rustic rescuer, instead of being either the action of some other participant, such as the drowning man, or else not an action at all, but something that happened to one or more of the participants? (b) What marks the incident as the specific act of rescuing?

At this juncture, reasons and desires move to the center of the stage. The interpretive account we suggest is this. (a) The event is an action by our unpolished protagonist because it is caused, in part, by his desire. (b) It counts as the specific act of rescuing because his desire was to remove the other man from the waters in which he was visibly drowning.

Why declare in our interpretive explanation of this particular deed that it was caused by the agent's desires? We admit that we are not in a position to set out the causal account of how a man's desires might beget his deed. But we suggest a causal interpretation of the relation between his desire and the deed, on the ground that, unless the hookup between desire and deed is causal, it is an enigma. A persuasive argument for this view appears in Donald Davidson's important essay, "Actions, Reasons, and Causes." [1] Davidson writes:

> A person can have a reason for an action, and perform the action, and yet this reason not be the reason why he did it. Central to the relation between a reason and an action it explains is the idea that the agent performed the action *because* he had the reason.
>
> If . . . causal explanations are "wholly irrelevant to the understanding we seek" of human actions, then we are without an analysis of the 'because' in 'He did it because . . .', where we go on to name a reason.
>
> One way we can explain an event is by placing it in the context of its cause; cause and effect form the sort of pattern that explains the effect, in a sense of 'explain' that we understand as well as any. If reason and action illustrate a different pattern of explanation, that pattern must be identified.

It may be question-begging to incorporate into our interpretive explanation of an action the provision that the action was caused by the reasons the agent had for acting.

The question which may be begged is whether the *only* unproblematic account we can have of the connection between what someone did and his reasons is causal. At any rate, notice that even if we incorporate the causal link between reasons (i.e., desires and beliefs) and deed into our interpretive explanation of a deed, we have not yet given the causal explanation itself, of *how* reasons bring about this effect. Perhaps you name a cause when you name the reason, but you do not give any generalizations about the conditions under which reasons of this type will always issue in performances of this type.

Thus there is no absurdity in this interpretive explanation of the rescue as being, among other things, an effect of the rescuer's desire. A parallel case, which does not involve human action, will demonstrate why there is no absurdity in this procedure. Take the event of a person's skin becoming suntanned. An interpretive explanation of the tanning process would specify, *inter alia,* that the process results from exposure of the skin to sunlight. That is what it is to get a suntan. The condition of one's epidermis would not be a suntan if it were the effect of something else or if it were spontaneous. An "artificial suntan," resulting from exposure to an ultra-violet lamp, is no more a suntan than synthetic diamonds are diamonds. Furthermore, this interpretive explanation of suntan is not a causal explanation of how the sun's rays bring about changes in the pigmentation of one's skin.

If you accept this distinction, between making an interpretive explanation which names a cause for some event, and giving the causal explanation itself, then it really does not matter whether we can explain how a man's reasons or desires might cause him to act. For we have shown the compatibility between interpretive and causal explanation for what someone does, in terms of the very same elements, his reasons or desires.

Shall we leave the argument at this stage? It is not enough to suggest the interconnections between interpretive and

causal accounts of an occurrence. We should point out that
interpretive explanations are quite trivial if they only
inform us:

(1) that a particular incident was so-and-so's action because it resulted from the reasons he had for acting;
and

(2) that the incident was the specific act of X-ing because
so-and-so's desire was to X and he knew that he was
X-ing.

What should be added to an interpretive account? The
other things worth saying will also concern the agent's
reasons, but they will not concern the causal relation between reasons and deed. A final look at the untutored
rescuer will clarify this. Merely to assert that the episode he
figured in was his action because it resulted from his desire,
and that it was a rescue because the desire which produced it
was a desire to remove the other fellow from the water, is
to assert very little. A more helpful thing to say about the
man's desire would be that it is by reference to his desire
that the native himself understands his behavior, and that
his view of what he did, in terms of his desire, has a special
primacy for other people who report his action. In other
words, the native's performance fulfills a purpose or intention that he would acknowledge as his own. He would
describe what he was up to in terms of this purpose or
intention, if he had occasion to be candid with us. Furthermore, it is this description of his behavior—the one he is
disposed to give when he is open and truthful—which
makes what he did the kind of act it is, rather than some
different type. For instance, if we are unsure what he was up
to, we would ask about his reasons. Was one of his reasons
for hauling the swimmer from the water that he wanted to
kill the man himself? Was it his plan to cook the wretch
for dinner that evening? Did he expect that the fellow
would give him something? If so, then he did not exactly
rescue the swimmer.

The agent's description of what he did, in terms of his

reasons, is particularly indispensable when his performance appears to be marred in some way. How could you prove that he failed to get the other man out of the water unless you establish that he wanted to get the fellow out? If there was some error on the native's part—if, for example, the man he removed from the water was not drowning after all—then the false belief, which was among the native's reasons for acting, must be mentioned. It is in this sense that the agent's own description of his deed and his reasons is so crucial. If we describe the native's behavior as an act of rescuing a stricken bather, we assume that this is how he would describe it if he were candid. And if his description were at odds with ours, we would have to revise or withdraw ours.

These remarks about the primacy of the agent's description of his deed, in terms of his reasons, are woefully incomplete. All that counts for our argument, however, is that when you report someone's behavior as you think he understands it, the explanation you furnish is an interpretive rather than a causal one. The items you are concerned with—reasons and action—may be causally related. But the explanation you offer does not set forth the causal pattern to which these reasons and this act conform. Perhaps the agent does not know of any relevant causal uniformities. The description under which he knows the cause of his action probably does not appear in any accepted or promising causal law. The events or conditions to which his description of his reasons applies, may have to be described in different terms, perhaps in another terminology, before these events can figure in a causal explanation of what he did. Yet even if you must have recourse to the jargon of neurophysiology in order to give the causal explanation of how his reasons produced his deed, they are still causal factors.

Philosophical opponents of a science of man are vindicated to a certain extent by this conclusion. They were wrong in supposing that if a particular event is a human action, it is exempt from causal explanation; but they were right in maintaining that other forms of explanation are indispensable for our understanding of what people do. They were right in saying that when a man reveals his reasons for acting, he does not provide a causal explanation of his action. We add, however, that the agent may still have described things which are causes of his action, although the assertion that they are causes is a relatively unimportant part of the interpretive explanation of what he did.

Action Theory.

Recently, attempts have been made to characterize the difference between human actions and effects of events that befall us in terms of a distinctive notion of causality, called agent causality.[2] According to these attempts, an agent can be said to be acting if he is "causing an object to have a property," or "is bringing it about that *p*," or is "making something happen." However, none of these activities need to be construed in turn as the effect of something that we do first or of something that antecedently has happened to us.

According to this doctrine, we can intelligibly say, e.g., that by yelling at an intruder a housewife might cause him to dash away. What we should *not* say, is that in addition to causing his legs to move, a person might cause himself to walk, i.e., that he might bring about his own locomotion as an event distinct from causing his legs to move. The suggestion is that one's walking is not properly construed as the *effect* of moving one's legs, since it is the *same event* as moving one's legs. By causing one's legs to move, one walks. However, by the hypothesis of this argument the motion of one's legs is the *same event* as one's moving them, in a case like walking: they are contemporaneous and occupy the same region of space. Consequently, if one causes one's legs to move, one also *causes oneself to walk;* so it cannot be the case both that walking is the same event as moving one's legs and that one can cause his legs to move but not cause himself to walk.[3]

This argument shows that the doctrine of agent causality does not succeed in providing a notion of "the causes of action" sufficient to distinguish these causes from other kinds. For if a person can cause himself to act, either there must be an event distinct from the action which is its cause or else the action and the cause are the same event. In the former case, the causal event would have to be either something we do first, something that antecedently has happened to us, or some as yet undetermined kind of event that falls between these two classifications. If we adopted any of these alternatives, we would be confronted once more with all the difficulties of Hume's doctrine.[4] In case the action and the cause are the same event, nothing would be added to the statement that a person walked by saying that he *caused himself* to walk. Thus unless some use can be found for the expression "cause oneself to act" which is different from the expression "act," the doctrine of agent causality fails.

In the course of this argument, we observed that the two reports, "His legs moved" and "He moved his legs," although they refer to the same event, have a different meaning. Thus "His legs moved" is consistent with saying, "But he did not move them," whereas this would not be true of "He moved his legs." Perhaps the key to our problem lies in this consideration. It suggests that descriptions of actions may differ in *meaning* from descriptions of bodily motions where the former and the latter both *refer* to the same event. Only the former description *implies*, however, that the event contains an element of purpose or intention.

The importance of the notion of purpose or intention to the concept of action is widely recognized. Norman Malcolm, for example, has recently given the following list of conditions that a given case of behavior must satisfy in order to be an action: [5]

(1) the behavior satisfies certain standards or arrives at certain results.

(2) it is the agent's intention or purpose to meet these standards or achieve these results.

(3) the behavior occurs *because* of the corresponding intention or purpose.

However, for Malcolm, the connection between, e.g., *intending to* X and *X-ing*, cannot be contingent. "Part of what we *mean* by 'intending X'," he says, "is that, in the absence of interfering factors, it is followed by doing X." For this reason, Malcolm concludes that "intention is not, in Hume's sense, a 'causal' antecedent of behavior. . . ." If we agree with Malcolm's conclusion, it is difficult to interpret the third condition listed above. How can the behavior occur *because* of the intention, if the latter is not a causal factor? To deal with this question we must examine the concept of an intentional action more closely.

In general, to say that a person is performing a certain action may entail that a certain description of the motion of his body is true, yet this description would not serve as an answer to the question, What is he doing? As an example, consider the case of a man who is struck down by an automobile while crossing the street. Let us suppose that the man is not injured, and that the car which has felled him continues down the street as if the driver were unaware of any mishap. The victim, after picking himself up, runs after the car, a grim expression on his face. Suppose that he succeeds in stopping the car and that an altercation subsequently occurs between him and the driver of the car. Later, we are asked to testify concerning what happened, with the restriction that our testimony be confined to an eyewitness report of what the victim did after being hit by the car. If we testified only that we saw the man's body change position rapidly from the point at which it was felled to the point where the car was apprehended, but refused to testify that we saw the man doing something that appeared to be an attempt to overtake the car, our testimony would certainly be regarded as eccentric. Yet the description, "The man (intentionally or deliberately) ran after the car," is not logically implied by observational descriptions of the motions of his body.

How, then, could we justify our claim to have "seen" the man try to overtake the car? In general, the justification of a claim of this kind would require considering what the man would say in response to the question, What did you do upon being hit by the car and knocked down? if he were asked the question and were candid or had no ulterior motive for refusing to answer or for disguising his actions. Thus in saying that the man ran after the car, we presuppose that he would so describe his behavior if he were asked, were candid, and so on. A similar consideration applies to other cases of bodily motions which we classify as actions. The description that the agent is disposed to give of his bodily motions, or omissions, has a special or primary status in our concept of action. On the other hand, in describing a man's bodily motions, we attach no special importance to what *he* would say in response to a question about them. Indeed, the notion of one's body moving is compatible with it being impossible for one to describe it. This would be the case when a person falls downstairs after fainting and so loses consciousness.

If this account is on the right track, then descriptions of intentional actions are differentiated from descriptions of bodily motions not by the fact that the former contain a reference, say, to a peculiar kind of cause of the bodily motion, such as a volition, but by the fact that in reporting an action we take into account the mode of presentation of the bodily motion (or omission) as it appears to the agent or the person whose body is moving. Let us call this mode of presentation of the bodily motion to the agent *the description under which he moves* (or *acts*). The phrase *under which he moves* suggests that the agent is the primary or originating source of this description. Thus in describing an action, we must take into account what the agent would say about the motions of his body. When we describe a person's bodily motions as an action, we are not classifying his bodily motions as having been caused in a peculiar way, but supposing that what he would say about his bodily motions, the way he views them, or what he believes he is doing, would be essentially involved in describing his behavior. Since we are referring to dispositional properties of the agent, we can speak of the description under which an agent moves whether or not he utters that description to himself or to others.

What if the description that the agent is disposed to give of his bodily motion is not one that we would ordinarily classify as a description of an action? For example, a person who is running after a car might be disposed to describe the event as a mere motion of his body from one point to another. Alternatively, he might be disposed to use the language of physics, neurophysiology, and behavioral psychology to describe his actions. This possibility appears to confront us with a dilemma. Either we would have to admit that a description of a mere bodily motion or event may be counted as an action-description, or we would have to insist that an agent could not be correct in giving such a description of his behavior if he wished to inform someone about his action. If we adopted the first alternative, we would be unable to distinguish between an action-description and a description of a mere bodily motion, in terms of the agent's dispositions to describe his behavior. If we adopted the second alternative, we would need some independent reason for rejecting the agent's description in a case like the one imagined. Such an independent reason would be provided by a general property of action-description which would suffice to distinguish them from descriptions of bodily motions that are not actions. A hint of such a general property is contained in the claim, made earlier, that a description of an action describes the *mode of presentation* of the bodily motion to an agent. Thus an action-description does not merely tell us what sort of bodily motion is occurring, but also what *meaning* the bodily motion has for the agent. However, this is not sufficient, since bodily motions which are not actions can also appear under a certain description to an agent—for example, a person who, bound and gagged, is being carted to his execution. Thus not every description which an agent is disposed to give of his bodily motions is a description of an action, but only those that present the bodily motion as *fulfilling a purpose or intention that the agent would acknowledge as his own.*

This helps us to resolve the difficulty previously encountered in considering Malcolm's criteria for distinguishing actions from behavior in general. According to Malcolm, the agent's behavior occurs because of the agent's intention, but the latter is not a contingent, causal factor. But there is an incoherence in asserting that something occurs *because* of something else, and yet that the latter is not a causal factor. Our account avoids this difficulty by connecting the agent's intention or purpose, not with why his behavior occurs but with how he *understands* it, a very different proposition. For an agent can have a certain understanding of what he is doing while he is ignorant of many of the factors that played a role in bringing about his behavior. However, our account agrees with Malcolm's comment that purposive explanations of behavior must account for the behavior "under its intentional description for the agent." It is this latter notion which is crucial for the concept of purposive action.

We might think that there is a contradiction in saying that there is a description under which an agent acts, if the agent himself is unable to formulate it, or would revise his description if pressed, or is deceiving himself about his behavior. But what we have referred to as *the description the agent is disposed to give* is not necessarily immediately available, unique, or correct. Consider an analogous case. We normally assume that if we want to know a person's name, we can find out by asking that person. The answer that he actually gives us is not necessarily correct; but in the absence of any reasons to believe that he is lying about his name, we would accept his testimony in preference to the testimony of another person. In reality the procedure is immensely more complicated, of course; but if people were not normally considered authorities about their own names, many of our familiar social practices would have to be discarded. A similar principle applies to people's actions.

Of course, we often classify cases of behavior as actions of a certain kind even when the classification does not correspond to any description under which the agent acted. For example, a tourist in a foreign country may be held responsible for infringing upon some religious taboo of whose existence and nature he is totally unaware. In this kind of case, the meaning of the behavior is not a meaning it has for the agent, but the meaning it has for a society, and the description under which the agent acts is not one which he would be disposed to give of his behavior, but only one which a member of that society would give of that type of behavior, in those kinds of circumstances. We may take account of this difficulty by augmenting our claim that a description of an action describes the behavior under its intentional description for the agent. What we shall say is that the description under which the agent acts must be either his own description or the description which a member of a certain society would typically give of that kind of behavior if it were his own behavior in the same kind of circumstances.

With respect to many cases of actions and bodily motions, therefore, the following propositions can now be seen to be compatible:

(1) the action is the same event as the bodily motion,

(2) a description of the action differs in meaning from the description of the identical bodily motion,

(3) action descriptions refer to the bodily motion (or omission) under its intentional description for the agent or for a member of a certain society.

VI

The Language of Social Science

Introduction.

As we saw in the preceding chapter, explanations of human conduct or social practices, such as we find in the social sciences and ordinary life, frequently involve hypotheses that refer (apparently) to what some individual or group *means* by its actions or social practices. This feature of explanation in social science has created a controversy concerning the logical structure and scientific status of such hypotheses.[1] The purpose of the present chapter is to explain some of the basic issues involved in this controversy, and to suggest some lines of thought for resolving it. In the next section, I shall introduce the notion of a *meaning hypothesis* in connection with meta-linguistic sentences whose truth-conditions are assumed to consist in what a speaker *means* by something he does, such as uttering a sentence; and I shall suggest that the standard use of *means* in the context of describing or explaining actions and social practices might be interpreted by analogy with this model.

As we shall see, empiricists hold either that meaning hypotheses and similar forms of discourse are not necessary for a social science or that by appropriate "syntactical transformations" of the sentences in which such hypotheses are ordinarily expressed, apparent references to what people mean by what they say or do can be eliminated from the language of science. I shall criticize these views on the grounds that hypotheses of the type in question are a characteristic feature of the social sciences as they exist, and that our aim as philosophers should be to understand and explain this feature rather than to attempt to analyze it away. The fact that admitting sentences of the type in question complicates the logical structure of our language does not, by itself, justify reductive or eliminative approaches, since it is not at all clear that a language which has been purged of these forms of expression would be capable of conveying every kind of empirical truth that we can express by natural language.[2]

In the course of the present and following chapters, we shall consider some of the main reasons which have been advanced by empiricists in recent years for rejecting or for requiring the transformation of ordinary discourse about human actions or social practices. In general, three types of reasons are considered: (a) those stemming from the apparent non-reducibility of the terms utilized in such discourse to descriptive concepts of behavior, or from the apparent non-definability of such terms by physicalistic or non-normative terms; (b) those stemming from the fact that many sentences descriptive of human actions or social practices are *intentional* and that many sentences used in the social sciences express *intentional* acts or states; (c) those stemming from the ability of language users to understand and distinguish sense from nonsense for a potential infinity of sentences of their language. Before proceeding, however, some further preliminary remarks must be made in order to clarify the claims advanced above.

Meaning Hypotheses.

In order to reduce our discussion to a compassable dimension, we shall take a model type of statement of the form "_____ means ***" and consider reasons that might be advanced for requiring the transformation or reduction of this type of statement to one of a different type which is allegedly more acceptable scientifically. The fundamental context in which we have occasion to invoke the notion of *means* is in reference to linguistic utterances of words or sentences of a natural language. Other uses of *means,* for example, in application to human actions or social practices, may be understood by analogy with this model.

Consider the utterance *"Le chien est gris"* spoken at a particular time and place, with particular phonemic and phonetic variations. Asked the *meaning* of this utterance, we might respond by saying that it is a token utterance of the sentence type *"Le chien est gris"* and *"Le chien est gris"* in French means *The dog is gray* in English. Our response has the form:

    (1) x is a token of S and S (in L) means p,

where x ranges over linguistic utterances, S is a sentence type of the language L, and 'p' is an English sentence.[3] Let us call sentences of the form (1) *meaning hypotheses* (or *translational hypotheses*). A sentence of this form evidently connects an instance of behavior—a linguistic utterance—with a sentence type of a language. If it can be shown that there is no valid reason for denying, *a priori,* that sentences like (1) may be part of a theory which as a whole is testable by appropriate observations, then we can infer by analogy that those explanations and knowledge-claims in the social sciences which refer to what some individual or group *means* by its actions or practices may also be parts of an empirically testable theory, and therefore be admissible into the language of science.

In calling conjunctive sentences like (1) *meaning hypotheses* I may seem to be blurring an important distinction between *pure semantics* and *pragmatics.* *Pure semantics* is concerned with the theory of meaning of linguistic expressions in general, in abstraction from the conditions and circumstances of utterance of such expressions by speakers of a language, while *pragmatics* is a name for the kind of inquiry which does concern itself with the conditions and circumstances of speaker utterance of sentences of particular languages. In fact, however, my term *meaning hypothesis* should not obscure this distinction. Meaning hypotheses should be classified as *belonging* to descriptive semantics, or pragmatics. My reason for ignoring the distinction between pure semantics and pragmatics in the present context is that sentences *like* (1) frequently are naïvely advanced by social scientists as empirical hypotheses posing no special conceptual problems. When this is done, social scientists are tacitly *presupposing* that an adequate pure semantic theory and a linguistic theory of particular natural languages is available for interpreting the latent content and structure of such hypotheses. Thus, in the context of discovery, a social investigator merely proceeds to learn the language of the society under study (if he does not already know it), and then to *observe* the conditions of social life in that society. He then asserts conclusions of the form "———— means ***", where "————" and "***" are words, sentences, actions or social practices or institutions, and he does not hesitate to offer empirical evidence to support his conclusions. My aim is to analyze *this* process, and to reveal some of the features relating to the logic of its justification. Thus my project is to investigate the scientific acceptability of meaning hypotheses within *pragmatics,* but my investigation does not belong to positive or scientific pragmatics.

One traditional source of difficulty about sentences like (1) is that they apparently license the following train of inference:

From: (1) S (in L) means p,
to: (2) S and 'p' have the same meaning,
to: (3) There is something which is the meaning of S and 'p'.

In other words, we seem to be conveyed by a natural process from (1), a meta-linguistic sentence, to (3) a sentence apparently about a non-linguistic entity. The question arises, what kind of non-linguistic entity could a sentence like (3) be about?

Traditionally, two sharply different answers have been offered to this question. According to one answer, *meanings* are to be identified with ideas in the mind, subjective entities knowable only by the person to whom they occur or in whose mind they belong. But this identification appears to make intersubjective knowledge of sentences like (1) impossible. In other words, it leads to solipsism. The traditional alternative answer is to identify *meanings* with abstract objects such as Platonic forms, i.e., objects which resemble concepts except that they are not tied down to expressions of any particular language. But the postulation of such abstract objects requires justification, and if the only evidence to support it is the fact that sentences like (1) are sometimes true, then this postulation cannot be used to explain the truth-conditions of these sentences. Let us call the first alternative *psychologism* and the second *platonism*.

Types of Behaviorism.

Conceivably, both platonism and psychologism might be avoided if some way were found of analyzing or otherwise accounting for the notion of *means* as it occurs in sentences like (1), in terms of what people do in the presence of an utterance and others similar to it, or in terms of the circumstances of utterance of similar tokens. For this would be to show that in the last analysis nothing more is referred to by sentences like (1) than intersubjectively observable things and properties.

In recent years attempts have been made to provide such a behavioral analysis of *means* by philosophers like Russell, Quine, Carnap, and Wittgenstein.[4] These attempts have taken different forms. The most direct approach, perhaps, is that of Russell and Carnap, who in different ways attempt to preserve the traditional terms of semantics, e.g., denotation, name, intension, etc., and to account in empiricistic and behavioristic terms for the traditional range of applicability and presumed explanatory power of statements containing these terms. Carnap once explicitly proposed a "behavioristic" reduction of "semantic intension [meaning] concepts," which we shall examine in the next section. A different kind of approach is taken by Quine, who denies the validity of many of the traditional terms and distinctions in semantics, e.g., the distinction between "analytic" and "synthetic" sentences, that is, sentences true by virtue of the meanings of the terms in them and sentences whose truth or falsity depends on contingent facts. In their place, Quine attempts to introduce a set of new, operationally defined technical terms with precisely delineated scope. Quine's approach has the advantage of relative precision, but his results may be judged meager and piecemeal. Wittgenstein, on the other hand, and the Oxford philosophers generally, have attempted to revolutionize the whole subject of semantics by questioning not only its traditional vocabulary, or the possibility of reconstructing its foundations, but also the standard methods of inquiry and criteria of acceptability which have commonly been employed in philosophical inquiry. Wittgenstein, for example, does not attempt to explain or analyze *means,* but to show that no problem about *means* remains when various "conceptual confusions" have been cleared away, e.g., the tendency to picture the *meaning* of an expression as an *object* of some kind.

While any of these *behavioral* theories would avoid the pitfalls of either platonism or psychologism, they have been subjected in recent years to intensive critical examination and in many instances have been found wanting. In general, two major kinds of objection have been lodged against all theories of this type, whether or not they propose to *analyze* the notion of *means* in terms of behavior.

One important type of objection concerns the question whether behavioral theories are capable in principle of providing an explanation of the kind of knowledge which a native speaker has of the meanings of the sentences of his language, for example, his ability to understand immediately and to produce a novel sentence of his language, one that need never have previously occurred in his experience or in anyone else's. According to Noam Chomsky, a contemporary linguist and philosopher, what is at stake is the possibility of explaining "the speaker's ability to produce and understand instantly new sentences that are not similar to those previously heard in any physically defined sense or in terms of any notion of frames or classes of elements, nor obtainable from them by any sort of 'generalization' known to psychology or philosophy." [5] For Chomsky, only by postulating "innate ideas and principles of various kinds that determine the form of the acquired knowledge in what may be a rather restricted and highly organized way" can satisfactory explanations of the native speaker's ability and competence be assured.[6]

The conception which underlies Chomsky's rejection of behavioral theories is that a natural language is "based on a system of rules determining the interpretation of its infinitely many sentences." Since a language makes "infinite use of finite means," it cannot consist of some set of mere routines, habits, or conditioned responses. To suppose otherwise is to confuse two quite distinct questions: (a) the speaker-hearer's knowledge of his language, i.e., his "competence," and (b) his actual use of language in a concrete situation, i.e., his "performance." Concerning this distinction, Chomsky says: "The problem for the linguist, as well as for the child learning the language, is to determine from the data of performance the underlying system of rules that has been mastered by the speaker-hearer and that he puts to use in actual performance." [7]

In so far as behavioristic theories claim to give an adequate account of how a native speaker comes to *acquire* knowledge of his language, and in so far as that account entails that the speaker must generate the rules of grammar inductively from the finite material of his experience, Chomsky is probably correct in rejecting them. But it does not follow that "the data of performance" is not relevant to *testing* the truth or falsehood of meaning hypotheses. For if Chomsky correctly characterizes the problem of the linguist, then it must be possible for a linguist to determine from "the data of performance" the "underlying system of rules" supposedly mastered by the speaker-listener. Despite what Chomsky says, there is one essential respect in which the problem for the linguist goes beyond that of the child in learning a language. Even if we must assume that the child has "innate knowledge" of a set of rules of grammar, the child's "knowledge" of these rules may remain implicit or virtual even after he acquires a grasp of the language; but the linguist must be in a position to *justify* his hypothesis that the system of rules he formulates as a grammatical theory really does express the system of rules whose mastery by the native speaker has been postulated. Or speaking more generally, the linguist must be in a position to justify his hypothesis that his analysis of the grammar of the language reproduces the meanings of the sentences of the language as those sentences would be understood by a native speaker. If the linguist is not a native speaker, it is difficult to see how he could provide a test of his hypothesis except by observations of speaker performance.

According to Chomsky, "linguistic theory is mentalistic, since it is concerned with discovering a mental reality underlying actual behavior." Indeed, he says that "observed use of language or hypothesized dispositions to respond, habits, and so on, may provide evidence as to the nature of this mental reality, but surely cannot constitute the actual subject matter of linguistics." [8] However, one who holds that there must be public or behavioral *criteria* of meaning is not committed to denying that there are any private mental processes; he is only committed to denying that sentences like (1) are true or false merely if they contingently correspond or fail to correspond to such mental processes. Thus while Chomsky's arguments may be fatal to standard behavioristic theories of how language is learned, they do not tend to show that there are no behavioral criteria of meaning.

A second type of objection which has been lodged against

all behavioral theories of *means* arises in connection with
the problem of analyzing sentences in indirect discourse,
what Russell called "propositional attitudes," e.g., a sentence like "John believes that the earth is round." [9] As we
shall see in the next section, R. M. Chisholm has shown
that Carnap's proposal for defining "semantical intension
concepts" (i.e., terms in the theory of meaning) in terms of
behavior, entailed a difficulty. The most plausible way
of avoiding the difficulty is to regard sentences like (1)
as themselves expressions of "propositional attitude," i.e.,
sentences having what Chisholm calls (after Brentano),
the characteristic or mark of "intentionality." We shall examine this issue in chapter VII. In any case, for Chisholm,
". . . means p" is to be analyzed, at least initially, as
". . . expresses t and t is about p," where t is a thought (a
person is the ultimate subject of such an analysandum). It
is because *thoughts* are intentional and can be about something that language can be intentional or meaningful, according to Chisholm.[10]

As we shall see, Chisholm's argument seems to hold
against standard empiricist attempts to provide a behavioral
analysis of *means* as a descriptive concept of intention in
natural languages. His argument, however, does not show
that *means* must be analyzed in terms of thoughts, in the
sense of private mental episodes in the life of a person.
Wilfred Sellars has argued that it is logically possible for
a language community to have sentences in its language
like (1) without having any terms for silent, conceptual
thinking.[11] This suggests that while there may be a synthetic, nomological connection between having thoughts
and using language, the concept of *means* may not be
logically dependent upon the concept of (privately) thinking about something. If so, the possibility remains open,
so far as a theory of meaning hypotheses is concerned, that
no reference to thoughts as opposed to overt episodes is
entailed by sentences like (1). In other words, there appears to be no reason why, in principle, observable behavior

unaccompanied by inner thoughts, cannot be *intentional* in Chisholm's sense; and we would expect to locate such intentional observable behavior precisely in a linguistic community, the model for which would be overt speech episodes.

Thus an empiricist does not have to argue that meaning hypotheses, in order to be testable, are equivalent to some set of descriptions of overt behavior. The condition which must be fulfilled is a weaker one, namely, that such hypotheses should belong to a theory which as a whole *implies* descriptions about behavior (and environment), i.e., if a certain set of descriptions about overt behavior were false, then the theory in question could not be true. Consequently, what he needs to show is that meaning hypotheses may be part of a theory which as a whole might imply facts about behavior. But this may be difficult to accomplish if Quine's conditions on a scientifically acceptable semantic theory must be met.

According to Quine, sentences are classes of physical events of a certain determinate kind; and any theory of meaningfulness of sentences must be expressible within the framework of an "extensional" logic for a physicalistic language, i.e., one which excludes mentalistic terms. Quine characterizes an "extensional context" informally in the following terms.[12] I shall refer to this formulation as (EC). (Nothing in my argument hangs on the fact that this formulation is informal.)

> (EC) A sentence which contains a sentence as a component clause is called an *extensional* context of that component sentence if, whenever you supplant the component by any sentence with the same extension, the compound remains unchanged in point of its own extension. In the special case where the sentences concerned are closed sentences, then, contexts are extensional if all substitutions of truths for true components and falsehoods for false components leave true contexts true and false ones false.

A context in which the truth-value of the whole sentence may be *altered* by replacing a part by another part which has the same reference or extension as the part replaced, may be called a *nonextensional* context of that part. In case the part replaced is a term, rather than a sentence, resulting in a similar alteration of the truth-value of the whole sentence, Quine calls the context "referentially opaque." [13] If the context is such that there is no alteration in the truth-value of the whole by any replacement of a term by another term having the same reference, then Quine calls the context "referentially transparent." For example, the sentence "Alexander is riding Bucephalus" is referentially transparent, since its truth-value is unaffected if we replace either of the names in this sentence by different names or descriptions referring to the same individuals (respectively). Thus, we might replace the name "Alexander" by the description "The son and heir of Philip of Macedon," and the name "Bucephalus" by the description "the favorite horse of Alexander the Great," without altering the truth-value of the original sentence. Later we shall consider some examples of sentences which are referentially opaque. If meaning hypotheses like (1) have the latter property and are thus nonextensional contexts, they are not, for Quine, admissible into a scientific language.

Carnap's Intensionalist Thesis.

In his paper, "Meaning and Synonymy in Natural Languages," Carnap referred to some objections that had been raised against "semantical intension concepts." [14] He noted that these objections concerned, "not so much any particular proposed explication, but the question of the very existence of the alleged explicanda. Especially *Quine's* criticism does not concern the formal correctness of the definitions in pure semantics; rather, he doubts whether there are any clear and fruitful corresponding pragmatical concepts which could serve as explicanda. That is why he demands these pragmatical concepts be shown to be scientifically legitimate by stating empirical, behavioristic criteria for them" (p. 234).

Carnap agreed that Quine's demand is a reasonable one, although he did not agree that "without this pragmatical substructure, the semantical intension concepts, even if formally correct, are arbitrary and without purpose." That is, Carnap did not think that "a semantical concept, in order to be fruitful, must necessarily possess a prior pragmatical counterpart," since it is "theoretically possible to demonstrate its fruitfulness through its application in the further development of language systems." Nevertheless, Carnap went on to say, if "for a given semantical concept there is already a familiar, though somewhat vague, corresponding pragmatical concept and if we are able to clarify the latter by describing an operational procedure for its application, then this may indeed be a simpler way for refuting the objections. . . ." Carnap then stated that the aim of his remarks was "to clarify the nature of the pragmatical concept of intension in natural languages and to outline a behavioristic, operational procedure for it" (p. 235). Thus Carnap proposed, in effect, to provide the foundation for a pragmatic theory that could be formulated in purely behavioristic, nonintrospective terms. In particular, he proposed to show how it is possible to test meaning hypotheses empirically, by defining the term *meaning* (or *intension*) in terms that refer solely to publicly observable behavior. This was brought out explicitly by Carnap when he described his argument as "the *intensionalist thesis* in pragmatics," i.e., the thesis that "the assignment of an intension is an empirical hypothesis which, like any other hypothesis in linguistics, can be tested by observations of language behavior" (p. 234).

Carnap's specific proposal regarding the general concept of intension was as follows: ". . . the intension of a predicate 'Q' for a speaker X is the general condition which an object y must fulfill in order for X to be willing to ascribe the predicate 'Q' to y." Carnap referred to this proposal as a "rough characterization," which would show both that "the general concept of the intension of any predicate in any language for any person at any time has a clear, empirically testable sense," and that "there is an empirical procedure for testing, by observations of linguistic behavior, a hypothesis concerning the intension of a predicate . . . for a speaker" (p. 242). Carnap also suggested that other controversial terms of the theory of meaning, e.g., the term *analytic,* could be defined in terms of intension, taking the latter as primitive.

Roderick Chisholm, in a paper commenting on Carnap's pragmatic meaning analysis, offered a reason for saying that Carnap's proposal for defining the concept of intension in natural language required "the addition of a psychological, or semantical, term which cannot be defined in terms which Carnap allows himself," i.e., in descriptive terms referring exclusively to speaker behavior. Chisholm uses the term *psychological* in a sense which is opposed to *behavioral.* Thus Chisholm, in effect, offered a reason for being sceptical of Carnap's attempt to provide a behavioristic explication of the concept of the intension of any predicate in any language for any person at any time.[15]

Carnap's definition of 'intension' is adequate only if it allows us to say of Karl, who speaks German, that an object y fulfills the intension of '*Hund*' for Karl if and only if y is a dog. Let us consider a situation in which Karl *mistakes* something for a dog. In this case, Karl would be willing to give an affirmative response to the question '*Hund?*' Hence the fox fulfills the condition an object must fulfill for Karl to be willing to ascribe '*Hund*' to it. And therefore the definition is inadequate.

Perhaps we can assume that Karl is usually right when he takes something to be a dog: he is in the presence of a *fox.* And perhaps, therefore, we can say this: 'the intension of "*Hund*" for Karl is the general condition which, *more often than not,* an object y must fulfill in order for Karl to be willing to ascribe "*Hund*" to y.' But if the occasion we have considered was the only one on which Karl has been in the presence of a *fox,* then, according to the present suggestion, we must say, falsely, that the fox does *not* fulfill the intension of Karl's word *'Fuchs.'* Moreover, if Karl believes there are unicorns and, on the sole occasion when he thinks he sees one, mistakes a *horse* for a unicorn, then the present suggestion would require us to say, falsely, that the horse fulfills the intension, for Karl, of the word *'Einhorn.'*

Since Carnap's proposal involved these difficulties, Chisholm considered several different ways in which Carnap's definitions might be modified with consistent results. One of these ways was the following: "The intension of a predicate 'Q' for a speaker X is the general condition which X must *believe* an object y to fulfill in order for X to be willing to ascribe the predicate 'Q' to y." [16]

In a brief note replying to Chisholm's criticism, Carnap admitted that his original formulation was an over-simplification and said that, of the several ways Chisholm suggested for refining the analysis, he preferred the one cited above, i.e., "the one using the concept of belief." [17] Being unable to provide a satisfactory analysis of "belief" in strictly behavioristic terms, Carnap abandoned his original program of providing a strictly behavioristic definition for the semantical concept of intension as applied to natural languages and speaker behavior. In its place he suggested a new view of the whole problem: ". . . the basic concepts of pragmatics are best taken, not as behavioristically defined disposition concepts of the observation language, but as theoretical constructs in the theoretical language, introduced on the basis of postulates and connected with the observation language by rules of correspondence" (p. 248).

Carnap also spoke of the "urgent need for a system of theoretical pragmatics, not only for psychology and linguistics, but also for analytic philosophy. . . ." He recommended that investigations be restricted first to small groups of concepts, "e.g., those of belief, assertion, and utterance," and later be extended to include "all those concepts needed for discussions in the theory of knowledge and the methodology of science" (p. 250).

The principal difficulty in analyzing intension in terms of belief, for Carnap, was that there is no agreement "with respect to the question of the best form for belief-sentences in a formalized language of science" (p. 231). Admitting belief-sentences in indirect discourse, e.g., "John believes that the earth is round," may lead us to a form of platonism, according to which "a belief must be construed as a relation between a person and a proposition," and to a form of semantic analysis "according to which an expression has infinitely many senses depending on the text" (p. 232). Even if these consequences can be avoided, sentences about believing "are nonextensional." Although Carnap viewed these complications as unwelcome and to be avoided if possible, he did not flatly reject the possibility that the "formalized language of science" must include sentences in indirect discourse. Nor did he deny that such sentences may belong to an empirically testable theory. Regarding the use of nonextensional sentences, Carnap said "I do not think that there is any compelling reason for avoiding the use of an intensional language for science, because such a language can be completely translated into an extensional one. . ." (p. 249).

Although Carnap abandoned his original aim of achieving a definition of "intension" in strictly behavioristic terms, his revised view that the assignment of an intension in a particular case is an empirical hypothesis belonging to a theory, which cannot be tested apart from that theory, is essentially sound.

Frege's Intensionalism.

Now consider a language specified as adequate for science whose logical features are construed in accordance with a platonistic semantics, such as Frege's theory of sense and reference.[18] Any semantics of this kind will essentially distinguish between two kinds of nonlinguistic meaning entities (denotata) called *senses* (intensions, propositions), and *references* (extensions, truth-values).

Let us suppose that in this language sentences occur which are such that the truth-value or reference of the whole can be altered by replacing a part by another part which, if they occurred in isolation, we would say referred to the same things or had the same reference. It does *not* follow that such sentences are nonextensional by Quine's criterion (EC). For we may hold that such an alteration in truth-value occurs only because *in that context,* the parts in question do *not* have the same reference or extension. To explain:

According to a theory of sense and reference, a term or sentence may denote either *what its sense determines* or it may denote *its sense.* In a so-called extensional context, a term or sentence denotes what its sense determines; in a so-called nonextensional context, it denotes its sense. For example:

(a) Oedipus believes (at time t) that the husband of Jocasta (at t) is ruling Thebes.

(b) The husband of Jocasta (at t) = the slayer of Laius.

(c) Oedipus believes (at t) that the slayer of Laius is ruling Thebes.

According to the play of Sophocles, (a) and (b) are true and (c) is false. That is, Oedipus does not know or believe (at t) that he is the slayer of Laius, although he knows that he is the husband of Jocasta. The missing facts, which Oedipus discovers in the course of the drama, are that he is the slayer of Laius, Laius is the former husband of Jocasta, and he (Oedipus) is the offspring of Laius and Jocasta. Thus Oedipus discovered that he slew his father and married his mother. The fact that (c) does not follow from (a) and (b) is a paradigm case of a so-called extensionality failure. On the other hand, the fact that any argument from (a) and (b) as premises to (c) as conclusion would be invalid, is entirely consistent with our intuitions about belief-contexts.

According to a theory of sense and reference, the singular terms in (b) will have the same reference (i.e., what their senses determine) but different senses. That they do have the same reference is indicated by the fact that both descriptions are satisfied by one and only one person, viz., Oedipus, if they are satisfied by any person at all. (Thus it is irrelevant whether "Oedipus" names a historical person.) That they have different senses (meanings, intensions) is indicated by the following considerations. Oedipus understands the terms and sentences employed in these contexts and knows how to use them correctly and how to distinguish between valid and invalid inferences involving them. Yet, while he knows these things, and while he knows (at t) that he is the husband of Jocasta and that he is ruling Thebes, he does not know or believe (at t) that *the slayer of Laius* is ruling Thebes.

According to our theory, "the slayer of Laius" as it occurs in (c) does not refer to *Oedipus,* but to the *sense* that "the slayer of Laius" has as it occurs in (b). Thus, in denying that (c) follows from (a) and (b), we do *not* imply that (a) and (c) are nonextensional contexts by Quine's criterion (EC). That is, according to a semantics of sense and reference, the components in question do *not* have the same extension (reference) in both (a) and (c). Hence, on this interpretation, (a) and (c) do satisfy (EC), i.e., they do not fail to satisfy it, so if satisfying (EC) is sufficient for calling a context extensional or referentially transparent, then (a) and (c) may have these properties. Furthermore, since (c) does not in fact follow logically from (a) and (b), the hypothesis that "the slayer of Laius" as it occurs in (c) does *not* have the same reference as "the slayer of Laius" as it occurs in (b), is just as plausible as the contrary assumption. There is no vestige of "paradox" in this hypothesis, nor any conflict with our "intuitions" concerning belief-contexts.

Let us try to make this conclusion clearer. Recall that Quine says that a *sufficient* condition for saying that a context is extensional is the following: "All substitutions of truths for true components and falsehoods for false components leave true contexts true and false ones false." (We are here concerned only with closed sentences.) Now consider the following sentences.

(i) The husband of Jocasta is ruling Thebes.

(ii) The slayer of Laius is ruling Thebes.

Assume that both of these sentences are true and that the singular terms in them refer to the same individual: Oedipus. Now consider the sentence:

(iii) Oedipus believes (at t) that the husband of Jocasta is ruling Thebes.

Assume that this sentence is true. According to Frege's theory of sense and reference, the reference of (i) is *truth,* and similarly with the reference of (ii). But we cannot substitute (ii) in place of (i) as the latter occurs in (iii) without altering the truth-value of (iii). That is, if we make such a substitution, we get the false sentence:

(iv) Oedipus believes (at t) that the slayer of Laius is ruling Thebes.

But all we are entitled to conclude from this is that these sentences do not fall under Quine's sufficient condition for saying that a context is extensional. We are *not* entitled to conclude that (iii) is a nonextensional context merely because a sufficient condition for saying that a context is extensional does not apply. Now according to Frege's semantics, the *reference* of the expression "the husband of Jocasta is ruling Thebes" as it occurs in (iii) is *not* truth but the *sense,* that is, the *proposition,* expressed in (i). Since (i) and (ii) express different propositions [i.e., the truth of (i) is not necessary and sufficient for the truth of (ii)], what is referred to as the object of Oedipus' belief, namely the proposition, is different in (iv) from the object of Oedipus' belief in (iii). In other words, (ii) and (iv) describe two different beliefs, one of which Oedipus has (at t) and one of which he does not have. Hence (iii) and (iv) are not shown to be nonextensional by Quine's criterion. For convenience, however, we can continue to call such sentences nonextensional because the truth-value or reference of the whole *is* altered by these replacements, and because these replacements have the same reference when they occur in direct discourse, as in (i) or (ii). It would be better simply to refer to them as Frege did, namely as cases of indirect discourse. We could go on to show that extensionality can be preserved for sentences in indirect discourse, provided that we are careful to substitute only expressions having the same sense in contexts of indirect discourse.

A standard objection to adopting a semantics of sense and reference, in addition to Quine's objection that it commits us to the existence of intensional objects such as *senses,* is one stated earlier by Carnap. Namely, it commits us to a form of semantic analysis according to which an expression has infinitely many senses depending upon the text. This objection, however, does not apply to our version of the theory. In our version of the theory, when using belief and similar contexts, an expression *denotes its sense.* In Frege's original statement of the theory, an expression in these contexts was supposed to denote its *ordinary sense,* i.e., the sense that it would have in a so-called nonextensional context (direct discourse), *and* to acquire *a new and different sense.* Hence, with every reiteration of a nonextensional context, the original expression would acquire a different sense for each such iteration, leading to an infinite hierarchy of senses. This leads to the implausible conclusion that we must be able to learn an infinite number of senses for a given expression. By replacing Frege's original requirement and holding instead that in direct discourse an expression denotes what its sense determines, while in indirect discourse it denotes its sense, we avoid this consequence. An expression in indirect discourse will continue to have just the sense it has in direct discourse, regardless of how many iterations of indirect discourse may be involved.[19]

What this discussion shows is not that we should adopt a semantics of sense and reference in preference to other kinds, but that we *need* a semantic theory in order to determine whether occurrences of linguistic items do or do not have the same reference or extension in different contexts. Hence the thesis that the language of science should be *extensional* is ambiguous. According to Quine's semantics, this thesis entails that the language of science should be purged of belief—and similar contexts. According to a semantics of sense and reference, no such consequence follows. The *extensionality* of the language of science can be preserved while admitting belief-contexts into that language. Hence one kind of standard objection to the admissibility of indirect discourse into the language of science, is without foundation. Arguments based on the need to preserve the extensionality of scientific languages cannot be used to buttress "physicalism and behaviorism" in the philosophy of the behavioral or social sciences. Since there exist rival semantical theories as well as interestingly different kinds of formalizations of natural-language contexts, the question whether a particular context is extensional or not is relative to your choice of formalization and to the particular sort of semantical analysis you adopt.

VII

Scientific Psychology and Intentionality

The Problem of Intentionality.

We observed in chapter III that according to some empiricists there is no need to employ interpretive explanations in the social sciences, since explanatory principles for meaningful or purposive human action can be formulated in purely behavioristic, nonintrospective terms. By this, the empiricists intend us to understand that introspective or mentalistic terms can be eliminated completely from the language of science. Later, in chapter VI, we considered an attempt by an empiricist (Carnap) to define the term *meaning* as applied to linguistic expressions, in strictly behavioristic terms, and we saw that this attempt failed because an adequate definition seemed to require the use of some mentalistic term, such as the term *belief*. However, this then leaves open the possibility that the term *belief* can itself be defined behavioristically, and thus that the claim of these empiricists can ultimately be vindicated. In recent literature, this latter question has come to be known as "the problem of intentionality." Accordingly, we shall devote the present chapter to a consideration of this problem.

Wilfred Sellars, a contemporary philosopher who has made important contributions to the philosophy of mind, gives a succinct characterization of the problem of intentionality in the following passage: [1]

> ... one major strand ... of concern to the philosopher who
> wishes to locate the aims and methods of scientific psychol-

ogy...is known traditionally as the problem of 'intention-ality', that is to say, the problem of interpreting the status of the *reference* to objects and states of affairs, actual or possible, past, present or future, which is involved in the very meaning of the 'mentalistic' vocabulary of everyday life. Believing, desiring, intending, loving, hating, reason-ing, approving—indeed, all characteristically human states above the level of mere sensory consciousness—cannot be explicated without encountering such *reference* or *about-ness*. It lurks in such notions as that of 'behavioral' (as contrasted with 'geographical') environment, and in the non-technical use of such terms as 'goal', 'anticipatory', and 'expectancy' which have become technical terms in behavioristically oriented psychology. And while in their technical use they may be explicitly introduced in terms of observables pertaining to overt behavior which no more contain the notion of reference or aboutness than do the observables of, say, physical theory, the problem remains of the relation between concepts so constructed and the mentalistic vocabulary with which the enterprise began.

Sellars's description of the problem of intentionality dis-plays an interesting ambivalence. He first identifies it as "the problem of interpreting the status of the *reference* to objects . . . which is involved in the very meaning of the 'mentalistic' vocabulary of everyday life." For example, when we believe, *there is something* that we believe; when we desire, *there is something* that we desire; when we love or fear, *there is something* that we love or fear; and so on. The relevance of this problem to scientific psychology is that this "reference to objects" apparently does not consist in any physically measurable behavior, and yet it is en-countered in all "characteristically human states above the level of mere sensory consciousness," i.e., above the level of states such as feeling a pain, experiencing an itch, or enjoy-ing a pleasurable sensation.

On the other hand, Sellars says, the "technical terms in behavioristically oriented psychology" may be "explicitly introduced in terms of observables pertaining to overt be-havior" which, like the terms of physical theory, e.g., terms such as mass, energy, acceleration, neutron, etc., do not contain any notion of *reference* or *aboutness*.

Now if Sellars is right about this second point, a question that arises is why we should regard the problem of intentionality as one that is particularly relevant to scientific psychology. For his second point seems to imply that scientific or behavioral psychology can proceed, at least in principle, *without* having to employ any terms or concepts derived from "the mentalistic vocabulary of everyday life," i.e., terms such as believing, thinking, desiring, intending, and so on.

But Sellars seems to *deny* this consequence when he says that there is still a residual problem of "the relation between concepts so constructed and the mentalistic vocabulary with which the enterprise began." Presumably, the residual problem to which Sellars is referring is that of explicating the technical or constructed concepts of behavioral or scientific psychology, e.g., terms such as behavior, response, stimulus, and so on. The problem is to provide such explication, i.e., a set of rules for the consistent and selective application of such terms, without essentially or tacitly utilizing the "mentalistic vocabulary with which the enterprise began." If this mentalistic vocabulary were needed in order to define or explain the meaning of the technical terms of scientific psychology, i.e., if operational definitions and rules were insufficient as a guide to their use and application, then we shouldn't have succeeded in *eliminating* mentalistic terms or concepts from psychological theory. For the scientific psychologist would be tacitly or implicitly employing these mentalistic concepts in order to pick out the overt behaviors he wished to describe, explain, or predict; and these overt behaviors, or many of them, might be of interest to psychology only because they depend on referential mental states or dispositions which do not consist in any physically measurable behavior.

But now our understanding of the problem of intentionality has shifted in an interesting way. It is no longer merely the problem of "interpreting the status" of referential terms in "the mentalistic vocabulary of everyday life." It is the problem of whether we can possibly *discard* such terms, once the enterprise of behavioristically oriented psychology is underway, and replace them by a set of primitive terms which refer exclusively to *observables*.

In a series of recent papers, Roderick Chisholm has argued vigorously that this problem cannot be solved in the way the behaviorist would like.[2] Scientific psychology cannot make any significant headway without at least tacitly employing irreducibly mentalistic terms or concepts. According to Chisholm, if we wish to describe psychological subject matter, we must use intentional language or some kind of language that we do not have to use in describing merely physical phenomena. What Chisholm presumably means by this is that if we wish to describe psychological phenomena in the sense of *including in the description* their aspect of *aboutness* or *reference,* as Sellars calls it, then we must use intentional language. For it is clearly possible to describe some psychological phenomena without using any intentional terms. For example, the sentence "Jones is in pain" describes a psychological phenomenon, but this description does not imply that there is anything which is the *object* of Jones's pain. But it is not possible, apparently, to describe a fact such as *Jones believes that he is in pain* without using intentional language (or some kind of language that we do not have to use in describing physical phenomena). In brief, Chisholm's thesis is that if a scientific psychology is not to leave *aboutness* or *reference* out of account, it must employ intentional terms or concepts. Assuming that intentional terms cannot be defined or derived from a primitive set of observables or from the physicalistic language of natural science, Chisholm's thesis would imply that behavioristically oriented psychology can never develop a system of concepts adequate for dealing with "characteristically human states above the level of mere sensory consciousness."

Concerning this question, Sellars remarks interestingly: [3]

> Someone correctly and truly says, using the language of
> everyday life, 'Jones believes there is a round table in the
> room' ('There is a round table in his immediate behavioral
> environment'); and a (somewhat idealized) psychologist,
> using concepts which have been aseptically introduced on
> a basis of concepts pertaining to overt behavior, describes
> Jones by formulating the sentence 'S is in behavioral state
> ϕ.' In some sense the psychologist is describing the same
> situation as his commonsense counterpart. Now the situa-
> tion as described by the latter includes *aboutness* or *ref-
> erence*. Does the situation as described by the psychologist
> also include *aboutness* or *reference*? If so, it can only be
> because aboutness or reference is constructible out of the
> aseptic primitives to which he has restricted himself (to-
> gether, of course, with the resources of logic and mathe-
> matics).

The question is, in what sense precisely is the sentence "S is
in behavioral state ϕ" a description of the *same* situation as
the sentence "Jones believes there is a round table in the
room." According to Chisholm, these two sentences could
describe the same situation only if the term "behavioral
state ϕ" refers to the same kind of referential mental state
or disposition that we ordinarily refer to by the term
". . . believes. . . ." If the term "behavioral state ϕ" has a
different reference, then it cannot possibly be used to describe the *same* situation as the "commonsense counterpart."

However, let us ask how a psychologist might succeed in
constructing a set of technical terms which were non-intentional and adequate for describing *aboutness* or *reference*,
while limiting his resources to a set of primitive terms
referring exclusively to overt behavior. A sufficient condition, perhaps, would be the following: if the mentalistic
terms in ordinary usage were, in Sellars's words, "themselves
built, albeit with an open texture and an informal reliance
on the context of utterance more suitable to practical than
to theoretical purposes, out of behavioral primitives," then

the language of scientific psychology would simply be "more of the same" and "there could be no question of its leaving *reference* or *aboutness* out of its picture of human behavior." The gap between ordinary mentalistic discourse and "the deliberately contrived language of scientific psychology" would be bridged by showing that the terms of ordinary mentalistic discourse themselves could be constructed from behavioral primitives!

This theory, often called "philosophical behaviorism," has been ably expounded and defended in recent years by philosophers such as Gilbert Ryle and Norman Malcolm.[4] Much of the inspiration for this view derives from the later philosophy of Ludwig Wittgenstein. Philosophical behaviorism denies the traditional assumption, which was first made explicit by René Descartes in the seventeenth century, that our ordinary mentalistic or psychological concepts are *introspectively* derived from our own conscious experiences, i.e., experiences that we can attribute to others only because we are "conscious beings" in Descartes's sense.

It may be argued that the notion of an *observable* is ambiguous, since it may refer either to the kind of thing that can be observed by more than one person at a time, e.g., a tree or a table; or it may refer to the kind of event which is not capable of being observed by more than one person at a time, such as a person's *sensation* or *experience* of a tree or a table. In the nineteenth century, psychologists introduced the term *introspection* to describe the way in which each of us is supposed to be aware of his own experiences or sensations. However, it is doubtful that we can properly be said to *observe* our own experiences or sensations, or that there is any peculiar mode of experience referred to by the term *introspection*. We should rather say, as Descartes did, that the notion of an experience or sensation implies the existence of a *conscious* act or event (and perhaps even the existence of a being who *is* conscious).

According to Descartes, although we speak of "seeing light, hearing noise, feeling heat," etc. (all of which are modes of observation), in contexts where the light, the noise, the heat, are assumed to exist as real objects, we can have identically the same *experiences,* e.g., as of seeing light, hearing noise, feeling heat, when these objects are "unreal," e.g., when we are asleep and dreaming. But the experiences of seeing, hearing, feeling, etc., cannot be unreal, even if we are asleep and dreaming. Thus experiences or sensations can exist whether or not their *objects* are real, i.e., whether or not there are any *observables* in Sellars's sense. Descartes concluded from these and similar considerations that only the *experience* is "properly called my sensation; further, sensation, precisely so regarded, is nothing but an act of consciousness" (*Meditations,* II). In other words, a sensation is not an observable; it is a private mental event.

The relevance of these considerations to our preceding discussion is this: if experiences or sensations are nothing but "acts of consciousness," and if *reference* or *aboutness* is contained only in the structure of conscious acts, then they are also outside the class of things that can be observed. Descartes once attempted to define the term *conscious event* so as to take this aspect of "privacy of reference" into account:

> By the term 'conscious event' I understand everything that takes place within ourselves so that we are aware of it, insofar as it *is* an object of our awareness. And so not only acts of understanding, of will, of imagination, but even of sensation are here to be taken as conscious events. Suppose I say: *I see* (or *I am walking*) *therefore I exist.* If I take this to refer to a seeing (or walking) that is done by the body, then the conclusion is not absolutely certain; for, as often happens during sleep, I may think I am seeing though I do not open my eyes (or think I am walking though I do not change my place); and it may even be that I have no body. But if I take it to refer to the very sense or awareness itself of the seeing (or walking), then it is quite certain; for in that case it has regard to the mind, and it is the mind alone that has a sense or conscious experience of itself seeing (or walking). [*Principles of Philosophy,* I,9]

The crucial phrase is: ". . . it is the mind alone that has a sense or conscious experience of itself seeing (or walking) ." This does not mean, of course, that the mind "walks" or "sees" but that the primary or immediate *object* of reference is always something "mental."

In general, then, for Descartes, mentalistic concepts would have to be "built up" out of our conscious experiences. Since these experiences might exist in the absence of the body or any observables, without that fact affecting the certainty of our knowledge of them, the concepts we form of them could not possibly be derived from anything but the conscious experiences themselves. Thus they could not be derived in the way the philosophical behaviorist suggests.

Franz Brentano, the nineteenth-century psychologist and philosopher, once proposed a hypothesis which attempted to capture the Cartesian notion of a conscious experience in terms of a common property which all and only mental entities (acts, events, states) could possess.[5] He introduced the term *intentionality* to refer to this property. According to Brentano, every mental phenomenon was characterized by the fact that it contained an "inexistent object." For example, if I have the experience of seeing something, then whether I am asleep or awake, in either case there is something that is the object of my experience; and it was this that Brentano called the inexistent object. Brentano supposed that the property of intentionality was found not only in such states as believing, desiring, intending, and in general what Sellars refers to as "characteristically human states above the level of mere sensory consciousness," but also in states belonging to that level, such as being in pain. The property that Weber uses to define human actions in a social context, viz., *meaning* or *Sinn* would also be an example of what Brentano would call "the mental."

Chisholm's thesis, which we described briefly above, has some relation to Brentano's. Concerning the latter, Chisholm wrote that "the point of talking about 'intentionality' is not that there is a peculiar type of 'inexistent object'; it is rather that there is a type of psychological phenomenon which is unlike anything purely physical." [6] Brentano's hypothesis that there is a type of psychological phenomenon unlike anything purely physical is defended by him on *a priori* psychological or metaphysical grounds. Chisholm, however, has presented a linguistic version of the thesis. According to Chisholm, there is a " 'logical', 'grammatical', or 'linguistic' property" that psychological sentences have; this property may be characterized in terms of a specific set of "criteria," and these criteria are not satisfied by "sentences that do not have a psychological subject matter." [7]

Chisholm's Criteria of Intentionality.

This is not the place to review the history of Chisholm's attempts to formulate adequate criteria of intentional sentences. Instead, I shall freely adapt his original formulations of these criteria to my statement of the problem, in a way that hopefully will obviate some of the criticisms of his thesis which have appeared since his first paper on the subject. Instead of speaking merely of "intentional sentences," as Chisholm did, I shall speak of intentional *languages,* and I shall say that a language is intentional if it is capable of generating grammatically well-formed and meaningful sentences such that:

   (a)   the sentence is contingent, i.e., it is either true or false but neither logically true, analytic, tautological, nor self-contradictory;

   (b)   the sentence purports to describe some fact, event, or situation; and either:

   (c)   the sentence is "nonextensional" in Quine's sense, i.e., it is such that the replacement of a name or description occurring in that sentence by a different name or description which names or describes the same thing, may result in a sentence whose truth-value differs from that of the original sentence; or

   (d)   the sentence contains a referring name, description, or phrase such that whether there is or is not anything to which that name, description, or phrase refers is consistent with the sentence being true *and* consistent with the sentence being false.

These criteria may appear somewhat hard to understand but we can easily show how they are supposed to work by considering some examples. Thus English is an intentional language, since it may generate sentences like the following:

(i) "Wilma desires to marry a suitable male."
(ii) "Wilma says that there is a man hiding under her bed."
(iii) "Muriel is afraid of the man at the window."

Consider (i). That Wilma desires to marry a suitable male may be true, though there is no one whom she shall marry. Hence "Wilma desires to marry a suitable male" is intentional [by (a), (b), and (d)]. Similarly for (ii). That there is or is not a man hiding under Wilma's bed may be true or false whatever Wilma says about it. Hence "Wilma says that there is a man hiding under her bed" is intentional. Regarding (iii), that Muriel is afraid of the man at the window may be true, although the man at the window is none other than her husband, and Muriel is not afraid of her husband. Hence "Muriel is afraid of the man at the window" is intentional [by (a), (b), and (c)].

On the other hand, although it may be true that Jones, lacking any appendages, is not scratching his arm, it could not be true that he *is* scratching his arm. Moreover, whatever description or name we substitute for "Jones" in the sentence "Jones is scratching his arm," so long as it refers to Jones and no one else, the truth-value of the sentence remains unaffected. Hence "Jones is scratching his arm" is non-intentional. Sentences such as "Zeus is identical to Zeus" are non-intentional since they are logically or necessarily true. Further examples can be supplied by the reader.

Chisholm has argued that his criteria are adequate to provide a "mark" of the psychological, in the sense that any sentence which satisfies his criteria will be a psychological sentence or be concerned with a psychological subject matter. This is not true of the criteria as I have presented them; that is, there are non-psychological sentences that will satisfy my criteria. For example, the sentence "Possibly there will be an earthquake in California this year" seems to satisfy my criteria, although it is not in any obvious sense psychological. However, we are not concerned with this aspect of Chisholm's thesis. The reason I have presented these criteria is that they provide us with a fairly precise formulation of the thesis that the social sciences, including psychology, considered as sciences of human action, cannot be reduced to natural science; i.e., the thesis of Weber, Winch, Collingwood, and others, which we have dubbed *interpretationism*. For we can now express this thesis in the following terms: An intentional language, we can say, cannot be a natural scientific language, in the sense of a language which contains no terms or concepts except those that can be derived from a primitive set of observables, in Sellars's sense (leaving so-called theoretical terms out of account). Hence if the language of psychology and the social sciences must be an intentional language, then these departments of knowledge cannot be natural or physicalistic sciences, in the sense in which the behaviorist claims that they can be.

That this formulation of the problem is not arbitrary may be shown by considering Quine's criticism of Chisholm's thesis (Quine calls it "the Brentano thesis"). According to Quine, Chisholm's view is "that there is no breaking out of the intentional vocabulary by explaining its members in other terms." Quine seems to regard the thesis not as false but as trivial, as being valid if at all only in virtue of "idiomatic" or "parochial" features of our language. "One may accept the Brentano thesis," Quine writes, "either as showing the indispensability of intentional idioms and the importance of an autonomous science of intention, or as showing the indispensability of intentional idioms and the emptiness of a science of intention. My attitude, unlike Brentano's, is the second." By an "autonomous science of intention," Quine presumably means one that could not be conducted in accordance with the principles of methodological behaviorism, or one that needed to employ mentalistic terms in its explanations and theories.[8]

Now Quine's shoulder-shrugging attitude is unjustified if, as he also insists, the language of science must *exclude* "intentional idioms." As Bruce Aune has written: [9]

> According to distinctively empiricist philosophies of science, the language of scientific theory is ideally extensional, with no room for expressions with Chisholm's marks.... Chisholm's views about the irreducibly non-extensional character of discourse about psychological phenomena are extremely explosive. If the language of science *is* ideally extensional, Chisholm's view has the consequence that a science of psychology—to the extent that it is a science of the mental—is strictly impossible: there would be mental phenomena about which we could not possibly construct a proper science.

The problem that Aune is referring to might be put in the form of an argument as follows. There are mentalistic properties that we can know and describe in true sentences of natural language. Many of these sentences are intentional, and intentional sentences are nonextensional. However, any scientific language is ideally extensional, i.e., each of its sentences is extensional. So there are truths that we can know and express in natural language which cannot possibly be captured in a scientific language. Since at least some of these truths are psychological, there are psychological truths which can never be expressed in a scientific language.

Assuming that this argument is valid, then in order to solve the problem that it presents, we should have to find reasons for rejecting at least one of the following:

(i) There are irreducible mentalistic properties which we can know and describe in intentional sentences of natural language;

(ii) These mentalistic properties cannot be described in

extensional sentences, whether of natural or constructed languages;

(iii) A scientific language is ideally extensional.

If and only if all three of these propositions are true and
unambiguous does it follow that there cannot be a "science"
of the mental.

As we have seen in chapter VI, the standard empiricist
method of handling this problem is either to deny that there
are any mentalistic properties not identical to physical
properties, i.e., to reject (i) , or else to attack (ii) by showing
how mentalistic or intentional sentences can be translated
into "equivalent" extensional sentences which refer only
to physical or observable events or properties. The aim of
my discussion will be rather different. What I will try to
show is that since (ii) is ambiguous, i.e., since there is a
sense in which intentional sentences can be construed as
extensional sentences without requiring any transformation
or reduction of the intentional sentences, we can, if we like,
retain (i) and (iii) while rejecting (ii). This will leave the
door open to the possibility that there can be a (non-
behavioristic) science of the mental. If Chisholm's thesis
is true that a strictly behavioristic approach to the description and explanation of human action cannot possibly
succeed, then this possibility is important and worth ex-
ploration.

"Intentional" and "Intensional."

The reader should avoid confusion (if possible) in the
use of the two terms: "intentional" spelled with a *t* and
"intensional" spelled with an *s*. The second term, as we
found in chapter VI, belongs to semantics and is used to
describe sentences that are nonextensional in Quine's
sense. The first term belongs to psychology and is used to
describe the characteristic of psychological states of referring to or being about something not necessarily contained
in that state. Thus, the sentence, "Ponce de Leon looked
for the fountain of youth," is both *intentional* (spelled

with a *t*), and intensional (spelled with an *s*); while the sentence "Necessarily, whatever is blue is not red" is *intensional* (spelled with an *s*) but *not intentional* (spelled with a *t*). We must now explore the connection between rejecting or accepting *intensional* objects in semantics and rejecting or accepting *intentional* locutions in psychology. For this purpose I will once again resort to Quine.

Quine does not explicitly say that preserving the extensionality of the language of psychology is necessary in order for psychology to become a science; yet he does say that "the various familiar non-extensional idioms tend away from what best typifies the scientific spirit." [10] And in *Word and Object* Quine speaks of "banning intensional objects on scruples of extensionalism." [11] This remark suggests that in Quine's view there is some conflict between "admitting" intensional objects and preserving extensionalism. Quine then goes on to speak about "verbs of propositional attitude," this being another way of characterizing so-called intentional idioms.

> Ordinary language has its 'that' clauses, and such clauses (with 'that' as conjunction . . .) function grammatically as singular terms . . ., thus evidently purporting to designate something. Their purported objects are what the philosopher takes up and calls, subject to certain refinements, propositions. . . . Since a prominent use of the 'that' clauses is as grammatical objects of the so-called verbs of propositional attitude, we found ourselves taking propositions in particular as the things people believe, affirm, wish, etc. Russell's term 'propositional attitude' is a reminder that we are not first in so doing (p. 192).

Further along, Quine says:

> . . . it is the propositional attitudes above all . . . that clamor for positing propositions or the like (p. 202).

Since there is no doubting the existence of "the so-called verbs of propositional attitude," i.e., intentional locutions, and since these supply typically nonextensional contexts, and since the propositional attitudes "clamor for positing propositions," etc., as "the things people believe, affirm, wish, etc.," it follows that preserving extensionalism for the language of science requires "banning" the verbs of propositional attitude, i.e., the grammatical structures which purport to designate intensional objects such as propositions.

Quine's extensionalism evidently involves much more than merely a commitment to preserve logical *extensionality* for a scientific language. For, as we have seen in chapter VI, the logical extensionality of a language can be preserved without "banning" intensional objects such as propositions. In fact, as we saw, granting such intensional objects, we can interpret belief-contexts in a way that is consistent with Quine's characterization of an extensional context (EC), so that we can, if we like, include such contexts in an extensional language. Quine's extensionalism in fact includes his estimate of the degree of ontic economy involved in maintaining a scientific outlook. What Quine wants to preserve is not merely the extensionality of the language of science, but an extensionality which is uncommitted to intensional objects such as propositions, senses, attributes, intentional properties or states of affairs, and so on. If we now recall what Quine says about verbs of propositional attitude (quoted above), we can see that the problem which genuinely concerns him is the appearance, due to grammar, that the extensionality of scientific languages can be preserved for belief-contexts only by maneuvers that lead to *platonism*.[12] Quine is willing to tolerate such platonism so long as only *extensional* abstract objects such as *classes* are postulated; but he draws the line at the point where our language begins to commit us to the existence of *intensional* abstract objects such as Frege's senses or propositions.[13]

The Method of Paraphrase.

Let us briefly glance at Quine's prescription for treating intentional sentences. Recall that we are assuming that there are mentalistic truths which we can know and express in intentional sentences of a natural language, e.g., truths such as "Concerning Oliver B. Garrett, Chisholm believes that he is still in hiding from the police." These are truths which any putative psychological science must be able to express.

If we assume with Quine that such sentences do not satisfy minimal conditions for occurrence in a scientific language, then in order to insure that such truths as the above may be captured by a scientific language, we must be able to paraphrase them into extensionally equivalent sentences that are "referentially transparent" in Quine's sense, i.e., are such that phrases occurring as objects of psychological verbs either are eliminated completely or continue to have the same reference that they have when they occur in direct discourse. On these assumptions, then, intentional sentences expressing mentalistic truths must *each* be paraphrased into corresponding non-intentional sentences with similar grammatical components and no significant loss of meaning, i.e., no change in truth-conditions.

One who assumes that intentional sentences are non-extensional is therefore committed to faith in the efficacy of the method of paraphrase, as the only means of avoiding the consequence pointed out by Aune: that if the language of science is ideally extensional, then a science of the mental is strictly impossible. Since the method of paraphrase is piecemeal, practitioners apparently must depend on their logical ingenuity in order to insure that every possible intentional sentence expressing a mentalistic truth can be captured by a scientific language. This should strike us as a precarious foundation for a putative science of psychology.[14]

In any case, the claim that the method of paraphrase is the only acceptable method of preserving extensionality for a scientific language is evidently valid only on the assumption that certain linguistic constructions entail that certain sorts of objects, or alleged sorts of objects, exist; and that a scientific language must therefore be purified of constructions that pretend to make reference to unsatisfactory sorts of entities or states of affairs. This seems to introduce a certain metaphysical outlook as a condition for a scientific *language*. If this assumption is justified, then the method of paraphrase must derive its appeal, in part, from the promise that it will provide ontological decontamination and yet preserve the adequacy of scientific languages to generate all the possible true sentences. I have not tried to show that this promise is empty, but only that decontamination is not called for where there is no proof of infestation.

That there is no proof of infestation may be illustrated by recalling Carnap's approach to this question. In dealing with some objections brought against his attempt to provide a behavioral analysis of psychological terms, Carnap declared his willingness to admit belief-contexts into the language of science and thereby abandon the program of logical behaviorism. He thus was willing, in effect, to tolerate intensional objects considered as "theoretical constructs." Carnap was unwilling to refer to this position as platonism, since he denied that employing such theoretical constructs commits us to a metaphysical theory according to which there must exist real, abstract objects designated by such constructs. Quine, on the other hand, uses the term *platonism* (or intensionalism) to refer ambiguously either to a position such as Carnap's or to a metaphysical view such as Carnap rejects. I have been following Carnap in my use of the term *platonism;* thus, in my use of the term, to refer to a theory as *platonistic* is not necessarily to refer to it as a metaphysical theory.

Our discussion in chapter VI of Frege's theory of sense and reference shows that there exists an interpretation of intentional sentences such that Quine's characterization of an extensional context is satisfied by those sentences. Thus intentional sentences may be construed in such a way that they are extensional. By adopting a semantics of sense and reference, we can consistently say that these intentional or psychological sentences are extensional, and that mentalistic states, if there are such, can be described in extensional sentences whether of natural or constructed languages. If so, Quine, Chisholm, Aune, and other philosophers are wrong if they claim that extensionality failures necessarily are *implied* in saying correctly that a sentence is intentional. Whether intentional sentences imply extensionality failures is precisely what should be called in question, rather than taken for granted. (Another way of putting this point is to say that Quine's way of characterizing extensional contexts is not the only logically possible one.)

Let us illustrate this by our example: Muriel is afraid of the man at the window. If we assume, as Quine evidently would assume, that the phrase *the man at the window* has the same reference, as it occurs in this sentence, as *Muriel's husband,* then, since Muriel is not afraid of her husband, and since the man at the window is none other than her husband, there appears to be an extensionality failure. This is the way Quine, Chisholm, and Aune would take it. But Frege's approach would be quite different. According to Frege's theory, the phrase *the man at the window,* as it occurs in the above sentence, refers to its *sense* rather than to Muriel's husband. Frege's theory, then, tends to explain how it is possible for us to say meaningfully that Muriel is afraid of the man at the window, even though the man at the window is identical to her husband and she is not afraid of her husband. The reason is not just that Muriel does not know or believe that the man at the window is identical to Max, her husband. The point is that Muriel, though ignorant of the identity, understands or knows very well *what a man at the window is,* i.e., the sense of that expression (or thought). As Max Weber might say, what really concerns Muriel—the object of her fear—is the *meaning* (*Sinn*) of the "social" action of a man appearing unannounced at a bedroom window at night.

Conclusion.

We began by considering the *problem of intentionality* as a problem for a psychological science which hopes to explain the higher mental states. We saw that behavioristi-cally oriented psychology, in order to provide for a science of the mental, must be able to develop a language adequate for describing *intentional* situations, acts, or states, without departing from its self-imposed restriction of employing primitive terms that refer only to physically measurable or overt behavior. We considered both Chisholm's thesis that such an enterprise cannot possibly be successful, and Quine's claims that Chisholm's reservations are "baseless." We then argued that both views rested on the premises that any *science* of higher human states must be behavioral and that intentional sentences are not *extensional*. Concerning the latter premise, having shown in chapter VI that the ex-tensionality of a language can be preserved in different ways, relative to the type of semantic analysis you adopt, we applied this result to the problem of the present chapter. We showed that since there is an interpretation of intention-al sentences according to which these sentences are exten-sional, the presence of intentional sentences in a given language is compatible with it being *scientific*. We then pointed out that a psychological theory which permits intentional locutions or sentences is not therefore unscien-tific. Thus there is no reason to think that "the problem of intentionality" constitutes an *a priori* stumbling block to the development of a scientific psychology.

VIII

Translational Indeterminacy

Meaning Hypotheses Again.

In chapter VI the reader was asked to consider the utterance *"Le chien est gris"* spoken at a particular time and place, with particular phonemic and phonetic variations. It was pointed out that if we were asked the *meaning* of this utterance, we might respond by saying that it is a token of the sentence-type *"Le chien est gris"* which means, in French, *The dog is gray,* and that our response has the form:

(1) x is a token of S and S (in L) means p,

where x ranges over linguistic utterances, S is a sentence-type of the language L, and 'p' is an English sentence. We called sentences of the form (1) *meaning hypotheses* (or *translational hypotheses*), and we suggested that a meaning hypothesis evidently connects an instance of behavior—in this case, a linguistic utterance—with a sentence-type of a language. Now since x is an utterance, (1) evidently implies that the speaker of x means something by something he does, viz., uttering x. On the other hand, a sentence-type of a language may be said to have a meaning independently of particular utterances of tokens of that type by speakers of L. If a speaker *misuses* x, then (1) would not provide us with information about what the speaker *intended* to express by uttering x. So (1) should be augmented to include the provision that the speaker understood L and uttered x intentionally. Thus our meaning hypothesis, more fully expressed, will have the form:

(1)′ K understands L and uttered x intentionally;
     x is a token of S and S (in L) means p.

Now we can derive the conclusion that K meant p by uttering x. Presumably a linguist would gather data, in order to confirm semantical hypotheses like (1)′, by considering what speakers of L intend to express by uttering sentences like x. Although this kind of data-gathering belongs in the context of discovery, the linguist would first have to justify *pragmatical* hypotheses such as

(1)- (a) K uttered x in order to express that-p,

(where 'that-p' apparently refers to a linguistically neutral entity such as a proposition) in order to determine what speakers of L intend to express by uttering sentences like x. And in order to confirm hypotheses like (1) - (a) he would have to identify the referential terms in x, distinguish them from the syncategorematic terms, and establish synonymy relations between referential terms of L and his own language. Hypotheses about these relations would have to be confirmed, in turn, by considering the behavior of speakers of L and their beliefs, in the manner suggested by Chisholm:

(1) - (b) K *believes* that object y fulfills the general condition Q which makes K willing to ascribe the predicate 'Q' to y.

In addition, of course, various technical hypotheses of linguistics would have to be tested and confirmed before the linguist would be in a position to put together a grammar for L and subsequently a translation manual for rendering sentences of L into English.

The steps in this procedure which Quine singles out for attack are the introduction of linguistically neutral meaning entities such as propositions, as in (1) - (a), and the assumption, presupposed by (1) - (b), that synonymy relations between referential terms of non-related languages are objective matters of fact. Let us approach Quine's argument by considering how he proposes to establish the non-testable character of "analytical hypotheses" of translation, i.e., hypotheses which purport to state that different terms in non-related languages might have the same *reference.*

Quine's Translational Indeterminacy.

Quine's thesis of translational indeterminacy (TI) may be briefly stated in his own words as follows: [1]

> (TI) ... two systems of analytical hypotheses [may] fit the totality of verbal dispositions to perfection and yet conflict in their translations of certain sentences. . . (p. 78).

(TI) implies that two such systems may yield all the same predictions about the verbal behavior of native speakers while giving different, even conflicting, translations of certain native sentences. If so, conflicts in translations of these sentences are not conflicts in predictions about verbal behavior, such as sentences uttered.

Quine also argues that:

> (A) ... two systems of analytical hypotheses are, as wholes, equivalent so long as no verbal behavior makes any difference between them. . . (p. 78).

Combining (TI) and (A) we get the result that two equivalent systems of analytical hypotheses may conflict in their translations of certain sentences. That is, we may have two systems of analytical hypotheses, both of which are compatible with all the dispositions to verbal behavior of native speakers, yet such that one system assigns to native sentence N the English translation E while the other system assigns E' to N, and E and E' are not "intrasubjectively synonymous" for English speakers.

This result seems strange, but to suppose that it is logically impossible is to suppose that (TI) and (A) are inconsistent. But (TI) and (A) only seem to be inconsistent, Quine believes, because:

(a) . . . sentences are thought of as conveying meanings
      severally,

i.e., we think that a sentence has a meaning independently of
all the other sentences of a language; or because we believe
that:

(b) . . . the objective references of terms in different
      languages can be objectively compared (p. 79) .

Evidently, then, (TI) is not the fundamental conclusion
that Quine wants to establish, but is merely a means towards
demonstrating the falsity of (b) and the presuppositions of
(a), and hence the truth of:

(2) Unless pretty firmly and directly conditioned to sen-
    sory stimulation, a sentence S is meaningless except
    relative to its own theory; meaningless intertheoreti-
    cally (p. 24) .

However, the presuppositions of (a) are vague. Consider:
(a)' For every actual or possible token occurrence of a
     sentence-type of a language, there is a meaning
     (proposition) uniquely associated with it.
(a)' might be true, while it is false that:
(a)'' The meanings (propositions) uniquely associated
     with such token occurrences of sentence-types of a
     language are *conveyed* independently of their con-
     nections with other sentences of that language.
In other words, a token may be said to *have* a meaning in
the sense of expressing a proposition, without implying that
this meaning can be conveyed or understood by someone
who considers it in isolation, or who does not understand the
language to which it belongs as a token of a type. Only (a)'
is a presupposition of classical semantic theories, such as
Frege's or Carnap's. (a)'' seems counter-intuitive or false.
Moreover, if (a)' is true, then it is possible that token
occurrences of sentence-types of different languages might
be objectively compared in order to determine whether they
express the same or different propositions.
   Now given (a)', (b) and (TI) , then (A) must be false.

That is, conflicts in translation would be evidence that two such systems of analytical hypotheses are *not* equivalent, even if they did yield all the same predictions about the verbal behavior of native speakers. Given the falsehood of (a)′ and (b), (A) and (TI) are consistent, since on this assumption two or more sets of analytical hypotheses which yield all the same predictions about verbal behavior may well be equivalent.

Most classical semantic theories of the sort Quine rejects, e.g., Frege's theory of sense and reference, assume a principle such as *sense* determines *reference* (or *intension* determines *extension*). By the foregoing reasoning, therefore, (a)′, which concerns senses or intensions of sentences, is verifiable or testable only if (b) is true. That is, two sentences in different languages which express the same proposition must have the same reference or extension. But if the objective references of terms in different languages cannot be objectively compared, as Quine claims, then the hypothesis that two terms each belonging to a different language have the same sense or meaning, is devoid of empirical content. Thus, given that the proposition expressed by a sentence is a function of the senses of its logical components or terms, the hypothesis that two *sentences* each belonging to a different language have the same sense or meaning is devoid of empirical content. Therefore, the truth of (A), i.e., of Quine's hypothesis that if no verbal behavior makes any difference between two systems of analytical hypotheses they are equivalent, depends on the falsehood of (b).

In a different passage of *Word and Object*, Quine states a stronger version of translational indeterminacy:

> (TI)′ . . . rival systems of analytical hypotheses can conform to all speech dispositions within each of the languages concerned and yet dictate, in countless cases, utterly disparate translations; not mere mutual paraphrases, but translations each of which would be excluded by the other system of translation. Two such translations might even be

> patently contrary in truth value, provided there
> is no stimulation that would encourage assent to
> either (p. 74).

This version is stronger than (TI) because it pins the translational conflict down to truth-values. According to (TI)′, E and E′ may be such that they are authentic translations of N by different systems of analytical hypotheses even though contrary in truth-value, i.e., not merely lacking intrasubjective *synonymy* for speakers of E. Nevertheless, if (1) is true, the occurrence of such a situation would not be evidence that at least one of the rival systems of analytical hypotheses is incorrect.

Translational hypotheses are testable, according to Quine, only for sentences whose translations do not require analytical hypotheses as to the objective references of terms employed in them, i.e., only for translational hypotheses which do not imply or presuppose (b). We need not investigate the kinds of meaning hypotheses whose empirical character Quine accepts, since we are interested only in those which he classifies as indeterminate. Indeterminacy applies at the level of "standing sentences," e.g., "There is copper oxide in it," and their logical relations "at the level of quantification or beyond."

Quine does not attempt to construct examples of alternative translation "manuals" which would yield contrary translations compatibly with all the observable evidence. He rests his case instead on an analysis of the "nature of possible data and methods" of testing analytical hypotheses. An analytical hypothesis is so-called because the translation must be based on an alleged identity in the reference of the terms employed in the respective sentences of the different languages. Thus in order to accomplish the translation of such sentences, the latter must be *analyzed* into their logical components or terms. Analytical hypotheses must provide "an infinite semantic correlation of sentences" since the number of different sentences in each language is infinite, but the only observable data available to the translator consists of a finite stock of actually produced sentences and the "stimulus conditions" which "prompt" native utterances. A system of analytical hypotheses, therefore, must generate an infinite number of sentences whose translations cannot be verified independently of the particular set of analytical hypotheses which the translator has already assumed in order to translate the standing sentences that he has had occasion to observe.

An essential part of Quine's thesis is that analytical hypotheses are significantly worse off as regards testability than scientific hypotheses in other fields. The question arises whether he can maintain this view consistently with his interpretation of the logic of confirmation of scientific hypotheses in general:

> (3) ... we have no reason to suppose that man's surface irritations even unto eternity admit of any one systematization that is scientifically better or simpler than all possible others. It seems likelier, if only on account of symmetries or dualities, that countless alternative theories would be tied for first place (p. 23).

In other words, the number of alternative theories which are plausible candidates for systematizing our observations is unlimited, and no observation, or "surface irritation" of a human organism, can possibly provide grounds for rating one such theory above all others. This seems to suggest that translational indeterminacy is merely a logical consequence of applying (3) to the case of empirical linguistics. But Quine attempts to cleave analytical hypotheses from scientific hypotheses by the following wedge. He says that if there were, contrary to the view registered in (3):

> (4) ... an unknown but unique best total systematization ϕ of science conformable to the past, present, and future nerve-hits of mankind, so we might define the whole truth as that unknown ϕ, *still* we

> should not thereby have defined truth for actual
> single sentences. We could not say, derivatively,
> that any single sentence S is true, if it or a transla-
> tion belongs to ϕ, for there is in general no sense
> in equating a sentence of a theory ϕ with a sentence
> S given apart from ϕ (p. 23f.)

In other words, sentences can be said to be true or false and
hence meaningful only so far as they are parts of a theory or
system of such sentences. Thus even if (3) were false, it
would still be the case that "a sentence S is meaningless except relative to its own theory; meaningless intertheoretically." But an analytical hypothesis purports to provide
such an intertheoretical meaning in the form of a so-called
translational hypothesis; and, hence, asserting such an analytical hypothesis implies that a sentence S might be meaningful *outside* the context of its own theory. This could be
the case only if the translational hypothesis were part of a
theory which could be tested by observations of the verbal
behavior of speakers. But Quine has shown, as he believes,
that "the use of a word as an occasion sentence, however
determinate" (i.e., as the sort of sentence whose translation
can be tested by observations of behavior) "does not fix the
extension of the word as a term" (p. 53). Thus a native
who utters "Gavagai" as an occasion sentence may be observed and the sentence translated as "Lo, a rabbit," and
this translational hypothesis can be tested by reference to
physical events in the environment or organism of the
native. But the reference or extension of *gavagai* considered
as a term need not be the same as the reference or extension
of the English term *rabbit*. By *gavagai* considered as a term,
the native might be referring to rabbits, rabbit parts, a
temporal segment of a rabbit, the class of rabbits, etc., and
which of these different analytical hypotheses were correct
could not be determined by the behavioral evidence that
legitimized the translation of "Gavagai," i.e., the native
utterance considered as an occasion sentence. Hence alternative contrary hypotheses about the extension of a term in

native use are consistent with all the behavioral evidence that can be gathered. Since, therefore, rival systems of analytical hypotheses cannot be tested by observations of the verbal behavior of speakers, supposed differences in the meanings of the sentences implied by the rival systems of analytical hypotheses cannot be genuine differences. Rival systems of analytical hypotheses are not *different* theories because they are not really *theories;* there is nothing observable for them to be theories *about.* That is why an apparent confirmation or disconfirmation of a system of analytical hypotheses of translation is empirically meaningless, why Quine says "mishap is impossible."

To revert to classical semantics and to suppose that (a)' and hence (b) may nevertheless be true despite (TI)' is merely to evince a failure to understand this point, Quine believes. Thus he says:

> (5) ...it is a mistake to suppose that the notion of propositions as shared meanings clarifies the enterprise of translation. The totality of dispositions to speech behavior is compatible with alternative systems of sentence-to-sentence translation so unlike one another that translations of a standing sentence under two such systems can even differ in truth value. Were it not for this situation, we could hope *to define in behavioral terms* a general relation of sentence synonymy suited to translational needs, and *our objections to propositions themselves would thereby be dissipated.* Conversely, since the situation does obtain, the positing of propositions only obscures it. The notion of proposition seems to facilitate talk of translation precisely because it falsifies the nature of the enterprise. It fosters the pernicious illusion of there being a uniquely correct standard translation of eternal sentences (pp. 207–8 [My italics]).

Evidently, then, Quine's argument for translational indeterminacy is a step in a larger argument against presuppositions of classical theories of meaning. As applied to translational theory, the argument purports to show that there is no need to "posit" propositions or "other sentence meanings . . . as things shared somehow by foreign sentences and their translations" (p. 206). From the standpoint of classical semantics, however, Quine's concession that his objections to "propositions themselves" would be "dissipated" were it not for the "fact" of translational indeterminacy, is significant. Even if we grant that Quine's confidence in the thesis of translational indeterminacy is justified, it does not follow that finding a way of *defining* "in behavioral terms a general relation of sentence synonymy suited to translational needs" is the *only* way to legitimize the concept of propositions. This is rather an assumption. This assumption is justified from Quine's point of view, since the only other way of showing that analytical hypotheses might be confirmed would be the one suggested by Carnap, viz., to consider terms such as synonymy and proposition as *theoretical constructs* of translational theory (i.e., pragmatics), "implicitly defined" by the theory. Since Quine has already rejected the possibility that systems of analytical hypotheses are genuine theories, terms such as *synonymy* and *proposition* cannot be theoretical constructs.

Indeed, Quine presents an argument "against . . . the whole idea of positing propositions."

> (6) . . . insofar as we take such a posit seriously, we thereby concede meaning, however inscrutable, to a synonymy relation that can be defined in general for eternal sentences of distinct languages as follows: sentences are synonymous that mean the same proposition. We would then have to suppose that among all the alternative systems of analytical hypotheses of translation which are compatible with the totality of dispositions to verbal behavior on the part of the speakers of two languages, some are 'really' right and others wrong on behaviorally inscrutable grounds of propositional identity. Thus the conclusions reached [above] may of themselves be said implicitly to scout the whole notion of proposition, granted a generally scientific outlook (p. 205).

More recently, Quine has written: [2]

> (7) A notion having to do with language seems pecu-
> liarly unpromising if its relation to observable be-
> havior is obscure, for language is first and last a
> system of dispositions to observable behavior.

Whether language is a system of dispositions to observable
behavior—and nothing but that—is surely a question of
fact which it is the business of the science of linguistics to
answer. However, Quine's argument for (TI)'—i.e., for the
conclusion which implies that systems of analytical hypotheses cannot be treated as empirically testable theories—
must assume (7) as a *premise*. For only if language is
nothing but a system of dispositions to observable behavior
must evidence about behavior be decisive in testing analytical hypotheses, and the failure to be able to find such
evidence in principle *entails* that translational theory
cannot be empirical. Consequently, Quine's argument does
not tend to show the falsehood of (a)' or to "scout the
whole notion of proposition" unless (7) is true and known.
Since (7) is a premise of Quine's argument for (TI)', if
(7) is false or doubtful then we can construct a counter-
argument which takes (a)' and (b) as premises and argues
to the falsehood of (TI)' and hence to the falsehood of (7),
leaving Quine's other premises undisturbed. Since (7) is a
factual claim which cannot be settled *a priori,* it is at least
an open possibility for a linguistic theory not to assume it.

Indeed, Chomsky has rejected the suggestion that language can be regarded plausibly as a system of dispositions
to verbal behavior.[3] According to Chomsky, the ability of
ordinary language users to understand and distinguish
sense from nonsense for a potential infinity of sentences of
their language cannot be explained in accordance with any
known facts or principles of behavioristic psychology. If
Chomsky is right, then (7) may be doubted on empirical
grounds relating to speaker competence and performance.
Since (7) seems necessary in order to derive (TI)' and

since the latter has nothing to recommend it independently of the premises which apparently compel us to accept it, to cast doubt on any of these premises is to cast doubt on (TI)'.

Let us inquire whether (TI)' is vulnerable to other objections. As we have seen, (TI)' presupposes that the translator may employ logical principles; otherwise he could not know that translations contrary in truth-value might be sanctioned by rival systems of analytical hypotheses. Now if the validity of these logical principles were contingent on the existence of particular languages, then (TI)' would lack any particular significance, since in that case we could not assume the validity of the laws of logic across culturally divergent linguistic schemes, and (TI)' as well as its own contrary would follow trivially from this. Presumably, then, Quine would not want to hold that logical principles are contingent on the existence of particular languages or families of such languages. But now we have a dilemma. If logical principles are *about* languages or symbolic systems, then we must be able to explain how *they* can be meaningful and apply intertheoretically or across widely divergent conceptual schemes. Otherwise we must say that elementary logical principles might not be universally valid in every language.

The question, then, is how, according to Quine, logical principles can be universally valid and meaningful intertheoretically. Either (TI)' applies to linguistic formulations of logical principles or it does not. If it does, then there is "no sense" in asserting that elementary principles of logic might be valid across radically different languages or "conceptual schemes." But this consequence is absurd; elementary logical principles must be valid in anything that we can call a language. If (TI)' does not apply to linguistic formulations of logical principles, then why should such formulations be exempted in this way? Since Quine can give no reason for exempting them, he must accept the former consequence.

If positing propositions provides an alternative to this result, then we can construct an argument *for* such positing which is at least as strong as Quine's argument *against* it. Quine's argument from (7) to (TI)´ is an argument against (a)´ and (b), and therefore by (6) against the positing of propositions, "granting a scientific outlook." By the same method of reasoning, "granting a scientific outlook" (6), and taking the contradictory of (TI)´ as a premise, we have an equally strong argument against (7) and in favor of positing propositions—*an argument which must be valid if Quine's argument is valid.*

If so, the real issue which is raised by Quine's arguments for translational indeterminacy is not so much whether there are propositions, or whether propositions can be posited as theoretical constructs of pragmatics; but whether a pragmatics which distinguishes between two separate aspects of meaning: a linguistic aspect and a non-linguistic aspect, can employ terms that cannot be explicated strictly in terms of verbal behavior. Quine's own pragmatics certainly admits that there are both linguistic and non-linguistic meaning properties. For example, his notion of "stimulus meaning" is a non-linguistic meaning property. Quine wants to confine the class of non-linguistic meaning properties to those which consist in or can be construed in terms of observable behavior or dispositions to such behavior. But it is precisely this premise that needs justifying, and Quine offers no argument for it, beyond saying that it is required by a "scientific outlook." It is not so much a scientific as a *metaphysical* outlook that is required to support this premise. The metaphysical outlook may be connected with a scientific outlook in this respect: a scientific outlook requires that we not multiply kinds of entities beyond necessity. Thus if there is no need to posit propositions or other kinds of intensional objects, a scientific outlook will not posit them. What is missing from Quine's argument for translational indeterminacy is a convincing

argument that there is no need for a semantics or pragmatics to assume them.

To illustrate this point, let us assume that our linguist
is attempting to construct a grammar for native language N
and that he is employing a classical semantic theory as part
of a pragmatics in which (a)′ is a theorem or postulate.
Given (TI) but without assuming (TI)′ the analytical
hypotheses he needs to correlate terms of N with terms of
English will be under-determined by evidence concerning
native behavior and dispositions to behavior. Using Quine's
example, let the native term be *gavagai* and the linguist's
analytical hypothesis be that in N *gavagai* means rabbit,
if and only if native speakers are disposed to ascribe *gavagai*
to all and only the objects that they *believe* to be rabbits.
According to Quine, to make this kind of move is to
postulate "translational relations as somehow objectively
valid though indeterminate in principle relative to the
totality of speech dispositions." The above hypothesis has
the form of a *meaning hypothesis,* as we previously called it.

Now if (a)′ is true or acceptable, then token occurrences
of sentence-types of different languages might be objectively
compared in order to determine whether they express the
same or different propositions. But how can sentences belonging to divergent languages be compared in this way?
Even if we were to adopt a criterion such as *analytical
equivalence* in order to decide whether or not two sentences
of different languages express the same proposition, how
could we apply this criterion in the case of radical translation? How could we determine that the truth of one sentence
in language N is a necessary and sufficient condition for
the truth of a different sentence in language L?

If we assume that the linguist understands both of the
languages to which the sentences belong as types, then there
is no more difficulty in determining analytical equivalence
across languages than there is between different sentences of
the same language. Since the linguist must learn both
languages before he can propose a system of analytical hy-

potheses, this assumption is justified. Of course any procedure of assigning an identity of meaning between different
sentences of different languages is highly precarious and
fallible, but it does not follow that such assignments are
untestable in principle. Assumptions about the reference of
native terms would have to be tested by considering not
only native behavior but also native beliefs and intentions.
If so, translational theory would need to include hypotheses
in indirect discourse, or *meaning hypotheses,* as we have
called them, and hence the language of translational theory
would not conform to Quine's restrictions on a scientific
language. But as we have seen, conforming to these restrictions is not essential in order to preserve the scientific character of a theory.

Notes

Chapter I

1. See E. E. Evans-Pritchard, *Social Anthropology and Other Essays* (Glencoe, Ill., 1962); R. G. Collingwood, *The Idea of History* (Oxford, 1946), and F. A. Hayek, *The Counter-Revolution of Science* (New York, 1955), for interesting if somewhat critical accounts of eighteenth- and early nineteenth-century conceptions of social science.

2. For a more detailed account of this controversy, see "Societal Facts," by Maurice Mandelbaum, in *The British Journal of Sociology*, Vol. 6, No. 4, pp. 305–17.

3. See *The Poverty of Historicism*, by Karl R. Popper, 3rd edition (New York, 1964), for a contemporary treatment utilizing Mill's approach but critical of many tendencies of Mill's thought.

4. The best brief statement of Weber's theory of social science may be found in *The Theory of Social and Economic Organization* (New York, 1964), pp. 87–115.

5. See Popper, *Poverty*, p. 130, and Carl G. Hempel, *Aspects of Scientific Explanation* (New York, 1965), esp. pp. 155–71.

6. The term *interpretationism* was first introduced by Thelma Z. Lavine in "Knowledge as Interpretation," *Philosophy and Phenomenological Research*, Vol. 10, No. 4 (June 1950), pp. 526–39. Max Weber's methodological views derive from the tradition described by Lavine.

7. ". . . the specific meaning intended by the term *Verstehen* . . . implies a particular kind of understanding, applicable primarily to human behavior." Theodore Abel, "The Operation Called 'Verstehen'," in *American Journal of Sociology* 54 (1948–49): 211–18. See below, Ch. III, "Max Weber and Interpretive Sociology."

Chapter II

1. *A Treatise of Human Nature*, ed. L. A. Selby-Bigge (Oxford, 1888). My references follow Hume's system: Quotations from the Introduction are indicated by page number in lower case Roman numerals; those from the main body of the text are indicated by Book, Part, and section. For example: Book I, Part 1, section iii, is indicated by "(I. 1. iii)." Quotations from the Appendix are indicated by Arabic-numeral pagination corresponding to Selby-Bigge.

2. This foreshadows Hume's later distinction between "relations of

ideas" and "matters of fact." See Hume's *An Enquiry Concerning Human Understanding,* sect. vi.

3. See J. A. Robinson, "Hume's Two Definitions of 'Cause'," for a complete and thorough discussion of Hume's doctrine of causality. (*Philosophical Quarterly* 12 (1962): 162–71. Reprinted in *Hume, A Collection of Critical Essays,* ed. V. C. Chappell (New York, 1966), pp. 129–47.

4. See Donald Davidson's "Actions, Reasons, and Causes," *Journal of Philosophy* 60 (1963): 685–700, for a critical discussion of this problem, and a list of the main parties to the dispute.

5. But compare Weber's treatment of this question discussed below, Ch. III, "Max Weber and Interpretive Sociology." Weber tries to show how first-person psychological knowledge *can* be used by a social science.

6. Thus Mill writes: "The physical sciences are those which treat of the laws of matter and of all complex phenomena in so far as dependent upon the laws of matter. The mental or moral sciences are those which treat of the laws of mind and of all complex phenomena in so far as dependent upon the laws of mind." And in another context of the same essay, he writes: "The desires of man and the nature of the conduct to which they prompt him are within the reach of our observation. We can also observe what are the objects which excite those desires. The materials of this knowledge everyone can principally collect within himself. . . ." See "On the Definition of Political Economy," in *John Stuart Mill's Philosophy of Scientific Method,* ed. Ernest Nagel (New York, 1950), pp. 407–40.

7. See A. H. Basson, *David Hume* (Baltimore, 1958), pp. 113–25.

8. Weber makes a similar claim. See below, Ch. III, "Max Weber and Interpretive Sociology."

Chapter III

1. See Marx's "Theses on Feuerbach," in Karl Marx and Friedrich Engels, *Basic Writings on Politics and Philosophy,* ed. Lewis S. Feuer (New York, 1959).

2. Review of A. Labriola: "Essais sur la conception materialiste de l'histoire" in *Revue Philosophique* (December 1897).

3. *Karl Marx: Selected Writings in Sociology and Social Philosophy,* ed. T. B. Bottomore and Maximilien Rubel (New York, 1964), p. 32.

4. Max Weber, *The Protestant Ethic and the Spirit of Capitalism,* trans. Talcott Parsons (New York, 1958).

5. Max Weber, *The Theory of Social and Economic Organization,* trans. A. M. Henderson and Talcott Parsons (New York, 1964), pp. 87–115. All the quoted material in this section is derived from these pages.

6. Max Weber, *On the Methodology of the Social Sciences,* trans. and ed. E. A. Shils and H. A. Finch (New York, 1949).

7. For example, see Popper, *Poverty;* Hempel, *Scientific Explanation,* and Abel, *"Operation . . . 'Verstehen'."*

8. See U. P. Place, "The Concept of Heed," in *Essays in Philosophical Psychology,* ed. Donald F. Gustafson (New York, 1964) pp. 206–27, and Place's references.

9. Carl G. Hempel, "Typological Methods in the Social Sciences," in *Philosophy of the Social Sciences,* ed. Maurice Natanson (New York, 1963), p. 221 and p. 230.

10. Hempel's claim will be investigated in detail in chapters VI and VII.

11. By empiricists such as Hempel, Popper, and Abel.

Chapter IV

1. Peter Winch, *The Idea of a Social Science* (New York, 1963). Page references are indicated in parentheses after quoted passages.

2. David Hume, *An Enquiry Concerning Human Understanding,* ed. L. A. Selby-Bigge. Many editions.

3. Winch's rejection of private mental entities is based on a version of Wittgenstein's argument against the possibility of a "private language." See Winch, *Idea of Social Science,* pp. 24–40. Also: Wittgenstein, Ludwig, *Philosophical Investigations,* 2nd edition (Oxford, 1958).

4. See Ch. II, "Hume's Experimental Method of Reasoning."

5. R. G. Collingwood, *The Idea of History* (Oxford, 1946). See also: Alan Donagan, *The Later Philosophy of R. G. Collingwood* (Oxford, 1962), pp. 157f.

6. Hume's *Dialogues Concerning Natural Religion,* ed. Norman Kemp Smith (London, 1935) , p. 3.

7. From *Two Centuries of the Church of Scotland, 1707–1929,* by the Rev. A. J. Campbell, p. 28. Quoted by Norman Kemp Smith, Hume's *Dialogues,* p. 3.

Chapter V

1. Donald Davidson, "Actions, Reasons, and Causes," *Journal of Philosophy* 60 (1963): 691, 693, and 692.

2. For example, "Action, Reason and Purpose," by Daniel Bennett, *Journal of Philosophy,* Vol. 62, No. 4 (Feb. 18, 1965); *Action, Emotion and Will,* by Anthony Kenny (London, 1963); "The Descriptive Element in the Concept of Action," by Roderick M. Chisholm, *Journal of Philosophy,* Vol. 61, No. 20 (Oct. 29, 1964).

3. Credit for this argument is due Professor Irving Thalberg, Jr.

4. See Ch. II, "The Relation of Reason to Action."

5. Norman Malcolm, "Explaining Behavior," *Philosophical Review,* Vol. 76, No. 1 (January 1967), pp. 97–104.

Chapter VI

1. For an extensive discussion of the controversy, and a list of some of the main antagonists, see "Meaning and Action," by May Brodbeck, in *Philosophy of Science* 30 (1963), pp. 309–24. The thesis that Brodbeck supports is in conflict with mine.

2. See "Theories of Meaning and Learnable Languages," by Donald Davidson, in *Proceedings of the 1964 International Congress for Logic, Methodology and Philosophy of Science* (Amsterdam, 1965), pp. 390–91.

3. Here I have borrowed from Wilfred Sellars, "Intentionality and the Mental" and "Correspondence," in *Minnesota Studies in the Philosophy of Science,* Vol. 2, (Minneapolis, 1958) pp. 507–10, 521–39.
   ed. H. Feigl, M. Scriven, and G. Maxwell (Minneapolis: University of Minneapolis Press). © University of Minnesota, 1958.

4. Bertrand Russell, *An Inquiry into Meaning and Truth* (New York, 1940); Rudolf Carnap, *Meaning and Necessity,* 2nd edition, with supplements (Chicago, 1956); W. V. O. Quine, *From a Logical Point of View* (Cambridge, Mass., 1953) and *Word and Object* (Cambridge, Mass., 1960); Ludwig Wittgenstein, *Philosophical Investigations.*

5. Noam Chomsky, *Aspects of the Theory of Syntax* (Cambridge, Mass., 1965), Ch. 1. See also his "Review of Skinner's *Verbal Behavior,*" *Language* 35 (1959), pp. 26–58.

6. Chomsky, *Aspects,* Ch. 1.

7. *Ibid.*

8. *Ibid.*

9. See Russell's *Inquiry,* and Carnap's "Meaning and Synonymy in Natural Languages," in *Meaning and Necessity.*

10. See Chisholm's replies to Sellars in "Correspondence," *Minnesota Studies,* Vol. 2: 521–39.

11. Wilfred Sellars, "Empiricism and the Philosophy of Mind," *Minnesota Studies,* Vol. 1 (Minneapolis, 1956).

12. W. V. O. Quine, *Ways of Paradox* (New York, 1966), p. 227.

13. Quine, *From a Logical Point of View,* pp. 142–59.

14. Carnap, *Meaning and Necessity,* pp. 233–48. Page numbers of quoted passages are indicated in parentheses following the quotations.

15. Chisholm, Roderick M. "A Note on Carnap's Meaning Analysis," in *Philosophical Studies* 6 (1955), pp. 87–89.

16. *Ibid.*

17. Carnap, "On Some Concepts of Pragmatics," in *Meaning and Necessity,* pp. 248–50.

18. G. Frege, "Sense and Reference," in *Philosophical Writings of*

Gottlob Frege, ed. Peter Geach and Max Black (Oxford, 1960), pp. 56–78.

19. This revision of Frege's original theory of sense and reference is that of Terence D. Parsons in *The Elimination of Individual Concepts,* unpublished Ph.D. dissertation, Stanford University, 1966, p. 52. Parsons credits Michael Dummett with having originated a similar view in 1960.

Chapter VII

1. Sellars, "Intentionality and the Mental," pp. 507–10.
2. Roderick M. Chisholm, "Sentences about Believing," in *Minnesota Studies in the Philosophy of Science,* Vol. 2 (Minneapolis, 1958): 510–39. See also: *Perceiving* (Ithaca, N. Y., 1957), Ch. 11, and Chisholm's references.
3. Sellars, "Intentionality and the Mental," pp. 507–10. I am not suggesting, of course, that Sellars would endorse either philosophical behaviorism or cartesianism.
4. Gilbert Ryle, *The Concept of Mind* (London, 1949). Norman Malcolm, "Wittgenstein's *Philosophical Investigations,*" in *The Philosophical Review:* 63 (1954) 530–59.
5. Franz Brentano, "The Distinction Between Mental and Physical Phenomena," in *Realism and the Background of Phenomenology,* ed. R. M. Chisholm (Glencoe, Ill., 1960), pp. 39–61.
6. Chisholm, *Perceiving,* Ch. 11.
7. Chisholm, "On Some Psychological Concepts and the 'Logic' of Intentionality," in *Intentionality, Minds, and Perception,* ed. Hector-Neri Castañeda (Detroit, 1967), p. 11.
8. W. V. O. Quine, *Word and Object* (Cambridge, Mass., 1960) , p. 220.
9. Bruce Aune, *Knowledge, Mind, and Nature* (New York, 1967), pp. 198–99.
10. Quine, *Ways of Paradox,* pp. 228f. ". . . indirect discourse is . . . at variance with the characteristic objectivity of science. It is a subjective idiom. . . . indirect discourse reports the event in terms . . . of a subjective projection of oneself into the imagined state of mind of the speaker or writer in question. . . ."
11. Quine, *Word and Object,* p. 191. Page numbers of subsequent pages from this book are indicated in parentheses following the quoted material.
12. See Ch. VI, "Meaning Hypotheses."
13. Quine's views are aptly summarized in his essay, "The Scope and Language of Science," in *Ways of Paradox,* pp. 215–32.
14. See "Theories of Meaning and Learnable Languages," by Donald Davidson, in *Proceedings of the 1964 International Congress for Logic, Methodology and Philosophy of Science* (Amsterdam, 1965), pp. 390–91. According to Davidson, a language purified of indirect

discourse by the usual procedures of empiricists would not be a learnable language, since the kinds of syntactical transformation usually recommended result in a language that contains an infinite number of "semantically primitive predicates."

Chapter VIII

1. W. V. O. Quine, *Word and Object*, Ch. II, *passim*.
2. W. V. O. Quine, "On a Suggestion of Katz," *Journal of Philosophy* 64 (Feb. 2, 1967): p. 52.
3. Chomsky, *Aspects*, Ch. 1.

Suggested Reading

Brentano, Franz. "The Distinction between Mental and Physical Phenomena," in *Realism and the Background of Phenomenology*, ed. Roderick M. Chisholm. (New York: The Free Press of Glencoe, 1960), pp. 39–61. This classical essay is of fundamental importance for understanding present-day discussions in the philosophy of the social sciences.

Collingwood, R. G. *The Idea of History*. (Oxford: The University Press, 1946). See especially pp. 205–315 for Collingwood's arguments against the possibility of a "natural science" of history or society.

Evans-Pritchard, E. E. *Social Anthropology and Other Essays*. (New York: The Free Press of Glencoe, 1962). Provides an informative history of the development of anthropology and other social sciences since the eighteenth century, together with some influential philosophical reflections on the nature of social studies.

Löwith, Karl. *From Hegel to Nietzsche: The Revolution in Nineteenth-Century Thought*. (New York: Holt, Rinehart and Winston, 1964). An intellectual history explaining the influence of Hegel and Rousseau on Marx and subsequent thinkers. Indispensable reading for anyone who wishes to understand present-day developments in social philosophy.

Nagel, Ernest. *The Structure of Science*. (New York: Harcourt, Brace & World, Inc., 1961). See especially pp. 447ff. An authoritative work defending the thesis of the methodological unity of natural and social sciences.

Rudner, Richard S. *Philosophy of Social Science*. (New York: Prentice-Hall, Inc., 1966). An effective brief introduction to the philosophy of the social sciences written from a standpoint similar to Ernest Nagel's. Contains an especially valuable chapter on concept formation and theory construction in social science.

Weber, Max. *The Theory of Social and Economic Organization*. (New York: The Free Press of Glencoe, Paperback, 1964), pp. 87–115. Contains Weber's classical exposition of the method of

Verstehen (understanding) and its indispensability in social research.

Winch, Peter. *The Idea of a Social Science.* (New York: Humanities, 1963). A stimulating discussion of the relations of social science to philosophy.

Anthologies

Braybrooke, David. *Philosophical Problems of the Social Sciences.* (New York: The Macmillan Company, 1965). A brief selection of representative readings with a contemporary orientation.

Brodbeck, May. *Readings in the Philosophy of the Social Sciences.* (New York: The Macmillan Co., 1968). A comprehensive anthology emphasizing methodological problems and theories as they arise in positive social scientific research. Many of the selections are written by social scientists.

Krimerman, Leonard I., ed. *The Nature and Scope of Social Science: A Critical Anthology.* (New York: Appleton, 1969). Another comprehensive anthology emphasizing philosophical problems of the social sciences from the standpoint of the philosopher rather than that of the social scientist.

Natanson, Maurice, ed. *Philosophy of the Social Sciences.* (New York: Random House, 1963). Contains many selections from the phenomenological school of social thought, and pits them against selections from the writings of "naturalists" such as Ernest Nagel.

Selected Bibliography

Aune, Bruce, *Knowledge, Mind, and Nature* (New York: Random House, 1967).

Brodbeck, May, "Meaning and Action," *Philosophy of Science* 30 (1963), pp. 309–24.

Carnap, Rudolf, *Meaning and Necessity* (Chicago: Chicago University Press, 1947; 2nd ed., with supplements, 1956).

Chisholm, Roderick M., "A Note on Carnap's Meaning Analysis," *Philosophical Studies* 6 (1955), pp. 87–89.

————, *Perceiving* (Ithaca, N.Y.: Cornell University Press, 1957), Ch. 11 and Chisholm's references.

————, "Sentences about Believing" and "Correspondence," *Minnesota Studies in the Philosophy of Science,* Vol. II (Minneapolis: University of Minnesota Press, 1958), pp. 510–39.

Chomsky, Noam, *Aspects of the Theory of Syntax* (Cambridge, Mass.: MIT Press, 1965), Ch. 1.

————, "Review of Skinner's *Verbal Behavior,*" *Language* 35 (1959), pp. 26–58.

Popper, Karl R., *The Poverty of Historicism* (New York and Evanston: Harper & Row, 1964).

————, *The Logic of Scientific Discovery* (New York: Harper & Row, 1965).

————, *Conjectures and Refutations*: *The Growth of Scientific Knowledge* (New York and Evanston: Harper & Row, 1968).

Quine, W. Van O., *From a Logical Point of View* (Cambridge, Mass.: Harvard University Press, 1953).

————, *Word and Object* (Cambridge, Mass.: The Technology Press of the Massachusetts Institute of Technology, 1960).

Russell, Bertrand, *An Inquiry into Meaning and Truth* (New York: Norton, 1940).

Sellars, Wilfred, *Science, Perception and Reality* (London: Routledge and Kegan Paul, 1963).

————, "Intentionality and the Mental" and "Correspondence," *Minnesota Studies in the Philosophy of Science,* Vol. II (Minneapolis: University of Minnesota Press, 1958), pp. 507–10, 521–39.

von Wright, Georg Henrik, *Explanation and Understanding* (London: Routledge & Kegan Paul, 1971).

Wittgenstein, Ludwig, *Philosophical Investigations*, 2nd ed. (Oxford: Blackwell, 1958).

Index

Aboutness, 142–46
Actions
  action theory, explanation of, 113–19
  causal and interpretive explanations of, 101–13
  individual, 57
  of mind, 32–35
  purposive, 73
  relation of reason to, 35–39
  social, 57
"Actions, Reasons, and Causes" (Davidson), 109
Acts, intentional, 121
Agent causality, 113
Analytic, defined, 132
Analytical equivalence, 172
Aune, Bruce, 151, 155, 157

Behavioral sciences, 1
Behaviorism
  language and, 124–30
  logical, 9
Bottomore, T. B., 50
Brentano, Franz, 128, 147, 150

Calvin, John, 98
Carnap, Rudolph, 10, 124, 128, 138, 140, 156, 162
  intensionalist thesis of, 130–34
Causality, 29, 33
  agent, 113
  analysis of, 31–32

  in explanation of actions, 101–13
Chisholm, Roderick M., 128–29, 132–33, 143–44, 147–52, 156–58, 160
Chomsky, Noam, 126–27, 169
Collingwood, R. G., 86–88
Conscious event, 146
Context of discovery, 3
Context of justification, 3
Contiguity, 31
Criticism as moral science, 16

Davidson, Donald, 109
Descartes, René, 145–47
Deutsche Ideologie (Marx and Engels), 50
Dialogues Concerning Natural Religion (Hume), 98
Direct observational understanding, 60
Discovery, context of, 3
Durkheim, Emile, 7–8, 50–55, 78, 85

Empirical observation, 92
Empirical societal knowledge, 88–90
Empiricism, 3–4
Engels, Friedrich, 50
Enquiry Concerning Human Understanding (Hume), 76–77